THE PERSON OF CHRIST AND THE SPIRIT

Notes of Meetings in Washington, U.S.A.

1949

J. TAYLOR

Vol. 179

STOW HILL BIBLE AND TRACT DEPOT
5 FIFE ROAD · KINGSTON-ON-THAMES

Made and Printed in England by
Cooper & Budd, Ltd., London, S.E.15

CONTENTS

*Scripture quotations which differ from the Authorised Version
are from the New Translation by J. N. Darby.*

THE PERSON OF CHRIST AND THE SPIRIT (1)

JOHN 1 : 1–18 ; 1 JOHN 1 : 1–14

J.T. The thought in mind at this time is to look into the gospel of John, not as a whole, but the earlier chapters, beginning with chapter 1 and running on through chapter 7. In order to make as clear as possible what is in mind it may be said that the first chapter of John contemplates the *Person* of the Lord Jesus. It is in mind that we should compare this chapter with the first epistle of John ; not that we should read the whole epistle, but have it in our minds, because the feeling is that the brethren all need to be grounded in the gospel of John just now. It is a time when we need to recognise the authority of the Scriptures, and John affords us instruction as to that. In chapter 1 of John's gospel we read, " In the beginning *was* the Word." Now while everybody is familiar with that statement, perhaps we shall see presently that we are not so familiar with its import as we had thought, and that we need to compare it with other scriptures that bear on the sonship of Christ, on His Person. John says, by the Spirit, in the first chapter, " In the beginning was the Word, and the Word was with God, and the Word was God. . . . All things received being through him, and without him not one thing received being which has received being." And then it says, " In him was life," and that is the thought we have before us. Now comparing that with 1 John 1 : 1 to 4, we read : " *That* which *was* from the beginning " ; not *He* which was from the beginning, but, " *That* which was from the beginning."

These verses in John's epistle are read so that the brethren may have the facts before them. The pronoun here is in the neuter ; it is not the personal pronoun as in John's gospel, for it refers to a thing ; that is, to the eternal life. Now the brethren will not misunderstand me, but while the Person is in mind ; that is to say, " the eternal life " refers to Christ, yet eternal life is not a Person. Some years past, there were certain who regarded eternal life as a Person ; they spoke of the personality of eternal life, which was not accurate. Although the Person is in mind, yet the idea in John's epistle is eternal life, whereas in chapter 1 of John's gospel it is the *Word*, the *Logos*, a divine Person. Although in manhood, but still, nevertheless, He is a divine eternal Person. The epistle says, " *That* which was from the beginning," meaning the beginning of Christ down here, whereas of " the beginning," in John 1 we cannot say when it was ; it says simply " the beginning." " In the beginning was the Word, and the Word was with God, and the Word was God." It is a Person that is in mind, an eternal Person, and He is going to be spoken of in the gospel of John. But there was more to be said, and the three epistles had to be written to make clear that it was the eternal life that was in mind, that the saints should understand that this was eternal life, and that this life was *in* Christ ; " this life was in his Son." That Person could be seen and heard and handled here below. I suggest all that for the brethren to think over. It has been gone over many times, but I think we are still somewhat cloudy as to these great subjects, and the distinction between John's gospel and John's epistles.

J.S.Sr. Is Genesis 1 the beginning of operations ?

J.T. Just so. " In the beginning God created the heavens and the earth," that is a question of God's operations, but in John it says, " In the beginning *was* the Word," without any question of operations.

S.McC. Have you something specific in mind in

2

saying that there is something about the beginning in John 1 that we may not be so clear about, although we have thought we were fairly clear about it ?

J.T. Well, just what we have remarked, that the first chapter of Genesis is a question of operations, the operations of God. " In the beginning God created the heavens and the earth." In John's gospel it is not that, but " In the beginning was the Word." It is not what He is doing, but that *He is* there. And then He was with God, and He was God. After that we have the operations brought in, " all things were made by him."

S.McC. That would help us in that while through grace we have part *with Him* in many things there is a uniqueness about Christ, the Person of Christ, and about His sonship too, that we need to give greater attention to, do you think ?

J.T. I do, and therefore the order is as already remarked, " In the beginning *was* the Word," the *Logos* ; that is to say, the Person through whom God's mind is known to us. Whatever God may have to say is made known through that Person, that is to say, the Logos. That is the first thing. and then the second is that, " the Word was with God," the Logos was with God ; then that He " was God," which brings out that the Lord Jesus is God Himself. There are not two Gods, or three Gods ; there is only one God, and He is that God, and the Father is that God, and the Spirit is that God. There is one God but there are three Persons.

J.H.P. I was wondering whether you had in mind that we should appreciate more the glorious Person of Christ as set forth in the first verse or two of the gospel as distinct from His operations, and our knowing Him through His operations ?

J.T. We should proceed on these lines, which is the reason for suggesting the first eighteen verses of John's gospel. I would add another word to further clarify the position as to the Spirit and the place that we hope He shall have in our conversations. In chapter 7 it is said, " for the Spirit was not yet, because Jesus had not yet been glorified." That is to say, what we have primarily in mind now is the question of eternal life which is basic, and it refers to what is down here, because as we see in chapter 6 the bread comes down from heaven; whereas chapter 7 speaks of Jesus being glorified, and what happens as a consequence after that. When Christ goes to heaven, that is to say when He is glorified, then the Spirit comes; and that is the point to make clear. It is an important matter in the minds of the brethren generally throughout the world at the present time, and I am not at all leaving that out, but my thought for the moment is that the brethren need the thought of the Lord's sonship, the Person of Christ Himself, and then to understand something of eternal life in that Person. The first epistle of John opens up thoughts as to *the* eternal life. When we come to chapter 7 we shall consider the Spirit specially, although we shall have occasion to speak of Him before, in many respects; but chapter 7 distinctly speaks of Him as here because Jesus is glorified. Moreover in chapter 6 the Lord speaks of " ascending up where he was before." " What and if ye shall see the Son of man ascend up where he was before ? " We shall have to connect that with the scripture in chapter 7 as to Christ glorified; the receiving of the Spirit stands in that relation; whereas the thought of eternal life stands in relation to the Holy Spirit down here, and to Christ down here as He was in incarnation, and for forty days after His resurrection which is alluded to in John's epistle.

S.J.H. Is the thought that John's gospel shows that it necessitates a divine Person, such a One as we have referred to that we might have eternal life, but when we come to the epistle there is something

4

further, " that ye may *know* that ye have eternal life."

J.T. That is the idea exactly. First that ye might have it ; " God so loved the world, that he gave his only-begotten Son, that whosoever believes on him may not perish, but have eternal life." That is the gospel, but the epistle was written, " that ye may know that ye have eternal life," which is a very important point. How many know that ? How many know it consciously ? We are told in the epistle, " He that believes on the Son of God has the witness in himself," which alludes to the Spirit, that it is not a question of testimony by the evangelist, or of the gospel, but that the Spirit of God Himself is in the Christian.

E.A.L. In Genesis 24 we read, " And she had said to the servant, Who is the man that is walking in the fields to meet us ? And the servant said, That is my master." The word *that* there, implies that she had the knowledge of Isaac through the operations of the servant, the Spirit typically. Would that help in bringing out what has just been said ?

J.T. That is, the Spirit is the witness.

E.A.L. Yes, and He gives the bride the knowledge of the Lord Jesus, typified in Isaac. Thus He comes into this.

J.T. Very good, and that brings up another question that is burning with us, that is, that we must recognise the authority of all Scripture. Every Scripture is inspired of God. There are those who have somewhat reduced the level of the Old Testament, but the Lord intends, I believe, at this present time to remind us that the Scripture cannot be broken, it is one whole.

A.R. We get the same idea in Romans 8, the Spirit witnesses with our spirit that we are the children of God.

J.T. Yes, just so, witnesses *with our* spirit.

5

A.N.W. The Lord touches that point in His statement in John 7, that " He that believes on me, as the scripture has said, out of his belly shall flow rivers of living water." He takes the pains to say, " as the scripture has said."

J.T. That is good. I am glad you mentioned that, because it brings up the whole question as to the importance of the Old Testament scriptures in that the Lord Himself quotes them there, and yet you could hardly show exactly the part from which He quoted ; we cannot say definitely, and yet we have His word, which is enough. What we are saying tests us as to our faith, because things are on the basis of faith and that is what John is aiming at, believing, and believing what the Lord Jesus has said. His words are authoritative, also the Scriptures.

R.P. In John 17, speaking of eternal life, Jesus says to the Father, " that they should know thee, the only true God, and Jesus Christ whom thou hast sent." Does not eternal life involve the knowledge of divine Persons ?

J.T. You will remember that the same thought is found in the epistle of John ; where John says, " He is the true God and eternal life." That " He " is Christ. So that the Father is called the true God in John 17, and the Son is called the true God in chapter 5 of John's epistle.

H.B. " Ye search the scriptures, for ye think that in them ye have life eternal, and they it is which bear witness concerning me." That would relate to the Scriptures you speak of. The Lord gives full credit to those.

J.T. That is of prime importance at the present time, because even though it may not be said or formally asserted, there are many who think that the Old Testament is on a lower level than the New, whereas it is not.

T.N.W. In Acts 17 we read that the Bereans

searched the Scriptures daily. They would be the Old Testament scriptures, would they not ?

J.T.   Just so, and if you look at the beginning of Acts where the account is given of the introduction of Christianity you will find a constant allusion to the Scriptures.

S.J.H.   One would like to ask whether *Old Testament* is a scriptural title ? Has not the enemy used this title and said, It is old ?

J.T.   Perhaps so. It is not a testament in the ordinary sense in which that word is used ; it is a question of testimony ; the word *testament* is based on the idea of testimony. So that if we use the term, it means that we have a testimony in the Old Testament and that that testimony is to Christ ; " and they are they which testify of me," John 5 : 39. " And having begun from Moses and from all the prophets, he interpreted to them in all the scriptures the things concerning himself," Luke 24 : 27.

S.M.   In Acts 17 we read, " And according to Paul's custom he went in among them, and on three sabbaths reasoned with them from the scriptures, opening and laying down that the Christ must have suffered," etc.

J.T.   " Opening and laying down," just so ; the opening up of things and then the laying them down with authority ; that is the idea, the way we should read the Scriptures. A brother opens up something from his Bible, but then he is laying it down by the Spirit, and thus it is authoritative. I hope we have something of that here now.

W.A.T.   When the apostles went with the Lord through the cornfields, the Pharisees criticised ; they wanted to bring in bondage, and the scripture quoted by the Lord was from the Old Testament. " Have ye not read," suggests that the Old Testament is there to give the brethren liberty, especially in connection with addressing the Spirit ?

J.T. Yes. It does too, it does give liberty. It is wonderful really how liberty is coming in amongst the brethren on this very point, because the Lord is really resentful that we have been neglectful in this matter.

V.C.L. Peter refers to the Spirit of Christ in the prophets. He refers to the prophets and what they testified, he speaks of the Spirit of Christ that was in them, testifying to the sufferings of Christ, and the glory after these. Would that not help our minds to see the true value of the prophetic word in the Old Testament ?

J.T. Showing that it is the full divine thought of the Spirit of Christ which was in them. It is remarkable.

A.B. Would the apostle Peter in 2 Peter 1 : 21, be referring to the whole scope of Scripture, when he says that " holy men of God spake under the power of the Holy Spirit " ?

J.T. Just so. There were no Scriptures when the book of Acts was written except the Old Testament. The Spirit of God began immediately to quote the Old Testament ; to confirm what had happened.

A.B. The Lord says in Luke 16, " If they hear not Moses and the prophets, not even if one rise from among the dead will they be persuaded."

L.L.P. The Lord said as recorded in Luke 24 : 25, " O senseless and slow of heart to believe in all that the prophets have spoken ! " What you are stressing is helpful, because the Lord speaks in verse 44 of the same chapter, about Moses and the prophets and the Psalms. It seems to make it unmistakably the Old Testament scriptures.

J.T. Quite so. The whole of Luke 24 confirms what we have been saying, and I thought in referring to chapter 7 of John that that should be one thing

8

in our minds. But we do not want to be diverted from chapter 1. We read the eighteen verses which bring out the idea of the only-begotten Son who is in the bosom of the Father having declared the Father.

A.I. Do you distinguish between John 1 where it says, " He was in the beginning," and the epistle where it says, " That which was from the beginning" ?

J.T. Yes, because the pronoun in the epistle is the neuter pronoun " *that* " ; whereas in the first chapter of the gospel it is the personal pronoun, " *He* " ; it is the Person that is in mind. " In the beginning *was* the Word." It is not some thought about Him, it is the *Word* Himself. You cannot say what beginning that was, but we should let it have its full scope with us ; it is " *the beginning*." " The Word was with God," that is a further thought, and then, " the Word was God." What can we get greater than that ?

A.R. In John's epistle it is in relation to the incarnation.

J.T. It is the incarnation, it is the beginning of Christ as here in flesh, to be handled and seen, etc. ; and what was seen was eternal life, it was there with the evidence.

W.P. John 1 : 14, says " And the Word became flesh and dwelt among us." The beginning of the epistle would refer to the Word becoming flesh.

J.T. It is the same thing exactly historically, and we contemplate His glory.

Ques. Do I understand that the epistles were written before the gospel ?

J.T. It is generally so understood. Probably one of the last scriptures written was the gospel of John.

A.N.W. Does not Genesis 1 agree with verse 3 of our chapter ? " All things received being through him."

J.T.   Quite so ; it is very remarkable ; not one thing that was made, was made without Christ.

A.R.   John 1 : 2 is not in relation to anything at all.

J.T.   We are not told anything about it. We do well just to meditate upon it and leave it, and let it have its full place in our minds, I say, in our minds, because with the Word, it is a question of the mind, not of the affections.

S.J.H.   Is there a suggestion of counsel in it ? Would not the very name *Word* indicate that something is going to be conveyed ?

J.T.   That is the idea. The *Logos* as I understand from others, means what God *has* said or communicated, or *may* say, which covers the whole thing, the divine mind ; not simply the affections, but the whole mind of God.

L.H.B.   Does it carry with it the thought of authority ? You mentioned that earlier.

J.T.   It would indeed, it is God's authority.

B.W.   Does the *Word* as used in reference to Christ here have any link with the Old Testament Scriptures ? Has it any reference to His speaking in the Old Testament times ?

J.T.   Well, it might have. I would not deny that. " In the beginning " ; that is the great idea ; the greatest idea we can have as to the mind.

F.N.W.   The hymn was changed from, ' Thou art the everlasting Word ' to ' Thou art the blest, incarnate Word.'

J.T.   Well, it is rightly changed. " Thou art the blest, incarnate Word," states the truth of the whole matter.

R.P.   Would you say that Paul supports that when he says, " And he is before all," in Colossians 1, as he meditates on the glory of Christ's Person ? Would that antedate Genesis 1 ? He says, " And he is before all, and all things subsist together by him."

J.T. " By him," is instrumental. That confirms what we are saying.

S.McC. Is the thought in naming Him *the Word* to keep before us in these last days that, while the Person has come into a subordinate position which the revelation of God required, yet that Person is none less than God ; He is on equality with God, and He is God, and He was God ?

J.T. That is what one thought we ought to see very clearly, " In the beginning was the Word, and the Word was *with* God," that is, association between divine Persons. Then " the Word was God." There are not two Gods, but the Word has the same place as God Himself, in fact He is God.

Ques. Does that go back before time ?

J.T. Oh, it must be eternity. You cannot make a beginning to Christ as to His Person. In the beginning He *was*. The word *beginning* does not refer to Him at all, as to His Person, He is a divine eternal Person. He is God.

S.McC. As John's gospel is about to open up to us the economy of love in which divine Persons are to be viewed, it is important that at the start we should get this word before our minds as to the Person of Christ, is it not ?

J.T. That is what I had in mind.

A.N.W. So that as you said the *Logos*, the Word, is to be in our minds. So far as I recall it is not referred to outside the verses we have read in this gospel and in the opening verses of Luke. Does John then proceed to engage our affections with that Person ?

J.T. Well, no doubt he does, but it is really a question of the mind.

A.N.W. I was thinking how important it is to

hold that Person rightly in our minds, now presented as in love.

H.B. Is this title not mentioned in Revelation 19 ? It says there that His name is called The Word of God.

J.T. Yes, it is, the same word.

E.G.McA. Would not this first verse stamp as a lie all the statements made by men who say that Christ emanated from the Father and all that kind of thing that is in the creeds ?

J.T. Quite so. The creeds are all full of error. But we are dealing with the real facts as to the Lord's Person, and we cannot say too much in impressing the brethren, that we believe on the Lord Jesus Christ as God ; He is God.

G.H. In Revelation 22 the Lord says, " I am the Alpha and the Omega, the first and the last, the beginning and the end." What is the thought there ?

J.T. Well, it is simply what we are saying. The Alpha and the Omega refers to the Greek language, the beginning of it, and the end of it. That is, Christ is that, He is the beginning and the end, but personally He has no beginning and no end. That is our God ; and to refer again to the question of love, that is the God we love, I think now we had better keep to the question of mind, that our minds are to become intelligent, because our minds are not nearly active enough. There is the power of the Spirit, the Spirit has come in to act on our minds. Nobody can deal with the points set out by men ; they have not the truth ; but it is our business to have the truth and to insist on the truth. It is a question of the mind. God has given us a mind that we should know the truth. " Ye shall know the truth," the Lord says, " and the truth shall set you free."

J.H.P. So that these first two verses should be

kept in mind whenever we are reading the gospel of John.

J.T. That is what I am thinking. These eighteen verses are wonderful verses; we come now to verse 14, to what the Lord became. "The Word became flesh," speaking to us of the ability of a divine Person to change. The Word became something that He had not been before, not that He personally is something else, because He says, "Before Abraham was, I am." There is no change in Him, personally, but He has become something else. Why should He not? A divine Person can do that; He can become something else, and that something is flesh; hence He has taken flesh; "the Word became flesh and dwelt among us, and we have contemplated his glory." Well, there it is in these first fourteen verses; let us go in for that.

L.L.P. God says to Moses in his moment of hesitancy, "I AM THAT I AM," Exod. 3 : 14. Would that have any bearing on it?

J.T. That is Exodus coming into John, but it does not come up to John. That is Jehovah saying, that He is what He is, and of course we revel in that thought, but when we come to John's gospel we get a divine Person formally stating that in the beginning He was, and He was with God, and "the Word was with God, and the Word was God." That is a greater statement than the One in Exodus.

A.P. The greatness of the Person is emphasised in the opening verses of the first chapter of Hebrews, as well as here. The writer of that book also seems to have the greatness of the Person in mind. He says, "God having spoken in many parts and in many ways formerly to the fathers in the prophets, at the end of these days has spoken to us in Son, whom he has established heir of all things, by whom also he made the worlds; who being the effulgence of his glory and the expression of his substance, and upholding all things by the word of his power, having made by himself purification of sins, set himself down on the right hand of the greatness on high."

J.T.   We are reading Paul in the epistle to the Hebrews, as he is no doubt the author, and he is dealing with instrumentality, that is to say, God has an instrument that He is using, and that instrument is the Son ; it says, " God . . . has spoken in Son." It is God Himself that is acting, but God in Son.

S.J.H.   Is it important to keep those names in the right setting ?   It does not say, In the beginning was the Word and the Word was the Son ; it says " the Word was God."

J.T.   Just so.   We do get the Son in Hebrews, but it is not on the same level really as what we get in John 1 because in Hebrews it is a question of instrumentality as regards what God is doing.   He touches on the idea of the Son, that the Son is the instrument through which things are done, but it is God Himself that is doing the thing, though as the Son.   He is doing them as the Son.

A.D.   It is all in relation to how God is speaking, is it not, the different ones whom God has used in speaking ?

J.T.   That is right. He has spoken by the prophets, and now He is speaking " in the Son."   It brings out the greatness of the Speaker.

A.R.   In John 1 you do not get the incarnation until verse 14 ?

J.T.   Exactly.   Verse 14 is the beginning.   " And the Word became flesh," that is the beginning of things.   That of course leads up to John's epistle.

A.R.   So you really get sonship in verse 14 for the first time ?

J.T.   It says, " and we have contemplated his glory, a glory as of an only-begotten with a father," and then it goes on to speak of the only-begotten Son.   It is a question of the sonship of Christ.

A.R. Which helps us to understand the idea of the incarnation, does it not ? What was before that we do not know.

E.P. In the contemplation of the greatness of the Lord Jesus here, we are to hold the other divine Persons equally in our minds. Does the stressing of the greatness of Christ here as the Word help us as to this ?

J.T. Well, of course, " the Word was God ; " and therefore " God " as being all three Persons, the three Persons are included in that. It is not the Father, it is God, " the Word was God."

W.W.M. In speaking of our minds, have we to remember that there is such a thing as an uncreated sphere ; and that the operations in Genesis in the creation come from One, in the uncreated sphere ?

J.T. Very good, the word confirms that ; He is gone up beyond all the heavens ; that is, into an uncreated sphere.

Ques. How should we understand verse 4 of John 1, " In him was life, and the life was the light of men " ?

J.T. It is what is called a reciprocal proposition, that is to say, you can say the life was the light of men, or you can say the light of men is the life. It is to show that it is a question of men, not of angels, nor of any other beings. The life refers to men, and we are the men. That is to say, in Christ was light for men, and that light was life, and it is for men, which of course includes women ; it is a question of the human race. That is a wonderful thing that we may well dwell upon, that God selected men for the working out of all His thoughts.

Ques. He refers to the men later in the gospel, does He not, " the men that thou hast given me " ?

J.T. Quite so, but that is more a matter of development in men, that they are not children. But the word *men* by itself includes the whole race.

S.McC. It has been said that we are limited to the terms of the economy ; but while we are governed by the light of the economy, would not this scripture remind us that while the Lord Jesus and the Spirit are in the economy in a subordinate way, there is personally a greatness about them that we are not to forget ?

J.T. We should ever remember the word *mystery* ; " great is the mystery of piety." We hardly know what that means. I feel it for myself that I know so little about mystery. " Behold, I tell you a mystery," Paul says. We should be mysterious persons ; the world does not understand us at all. We know so much as we do because we are selected by God to have this knowledge, the knowledge of Himself. And so Paul says, I want you to know how much I know about mystery. That is what he says to the Ephesians. Well, I say, I do not know what Paul knew but I would like to. That is what I think we should have before us, this idea of mystery.

W.A.T. In that connection our minds should help us. It speaks of the mind of the Spirit.

J.T. Quite so.

Ques. " By whom also he made the worlds," Heb. 1 : 2. How are we to understand that ?

J.T. Well, that refers to instrumentality ; that is to say, it is God that is doing it, but it is really God in the economy, and God in the economy is using one of the Persons or two of Them. Certainly in Hebrews 1 it is the Son.

W.McK. What is the distinction between what we are reading here, " the Word was God," and 1 John 5, " He is the true God " ?

J.T. We have just been saying, that the same expression is found in John 17. The Father is said to be the true God there, but the Son is said to be the true God in John's epistle. Well, we have to accept that, it shows the mystery of the thing. I think we should understand the thought of mystery; we should be humble about it, and be ready for mystery, and for inscrutability. It says, " the mystery of piety (or godliness) is great, God has been manifested in flesh, has been justified in the Spirit, has appeared to angels, has been preached among the nations, has been believed on in the world, has been received up in glory." Well, these are wonderful things, they are a mystery, but they are known to piety. What do I know about them? That is what everyone should ask himself.

J.H.P. Would you say something on the sentence, " the Word was with God " ? You have spoken of " the Word was God."

J.T. Well, it is just to bring out the society, so to speak, the social feeling of the association between the Father and the Son, if we are to bring the economy into it. He was with God. *With* is a peculiar preposition; this Person called the Word or the Logos, He was with God, that is the idea of association of the Persons. The word *association* is the only one I can use to make it clear what existed between these Persons. But then the Spirit of God does not stop at that, He says, " the Word was God." In the Roman economy, as I understand, there were three emperors at one time all on the same level, all of the same importance. If one said anything the others said it. Well, that is used just as an illustration of what we are saying as to Deity, that the three Persons are equal, they are equal actually in Their abstract relations.

A.D. Would that bring in the thought of unity, " the Word was with God " ?

J.T. The word unity is not great enough.

A.N.W. I was thinking of the expression used by Mr. Darby, ' Distinctiveness of personality.'

J.T. We might say of ourselves that we are united or of one mind about things, but you cannot very well say that about divine Persons. The matter is too great for that.

F.N.W. Would it be more in order to connect the word unity with the economies into which God may have entered, whether in creation, or in the present economy ? We are speaking now of the association before any economy was entered upon.

J.T. Yes, and it is all abstract, it is a question of dealing with matters abstractly.

S.McC. So that the prepositions in these first eighteen verses are really unique, are they not ? The prepositions are divinely selected. You said years ago in regard to the controversy in connection with our Lord's sonship that the prepositions in these eighteen verses were like a sword guarding the Person of Christ, and the preposition ' *with* ' to which you have been referring involves what you have been saying—association.

J.T. That is so.

A.N.W. And is not the excellence of wisdom seen in the fact that it says, " In the beginning was the Word," not, In the beginning was the Son ?

J.T. Just so.

S.J.H. Do we understand then that there are three divine Persons known as the Father, the Son and the Holy Spirit, yet there is one God ?

J.T. Paul says, " Yet to us there is one God, the Father, of whom all things, and we for him ; and one Lord, Jesus Christ, by whom are all things, and we by him." We might add the Spirit, but the Spirit is not mentioned there ; though in truth He is there. Therefore there is nothing in that to militate against what we are saying.

S.J.H. In thinking of the Father then, it would not include the three Persons ?

J.T. Oh, no ; the Father is distinct as one Person, " one God, the Father." The Father there is viewed as God, but not as three Persons. God is entitled to that name and that is the way John generally uses the word *Father*.

Ques. Would it be right to say that these terms have their significance only in view of the incarnation?

J.T. Just so ; the incarnation makes it all very simple. God is pleased to make it simple for us, and yet we are feeling the need of learning the mysteries so as to understand inscrutability, to get some idea of inscrutability.

Ques. When the Lord says, " I and the Father are one," is that in relation to His operations here in the economy ?

J.T. Quite so, because what is in mind is what is being done.

V.C.L. Does not the use of certain terms such as the word *' beginning '* in verse 1 show the extraordinary grace of the Spirit of God to encourage us to understand as much as we can with our minds ?

J.T. That is right, and the Spirit of God is here this afternoon just to help us on these lines, and if we are kept in His mind we shall get help, because we are dealing with the greatest things, and we are to see how we can take them into our minds, being humble about it, and getting to God about it. Prayer is a great thing. Luke would go with John in regard to that, for Luke is constantly alluding to prayer ; he says of the Lord, that He prayed all night.

R.P. Would you say a little more as to the prepositions our brother referred to ?

J.T. You tell them, Mr. McC., about those prepositions.

S.McC. I am just thinking of what you yourself had drawn attention to in that article, " *The Names of Divine Persons*," which was a means of help to the whole assembly. You pointed out that the preposition *' with '* in verse 1 involved equality ; *' alongside of '* ; whereas the preposition *' in '* in verse 18, " *in* the bosom of the Father," indicates that the position was arrived at by motion towards, and this alludes to the Lord in manhood, not in the pre-incarnate conditions of Deity.

R.P. That is very beautiful.

J.T. Yes, it is very beautiful, and we should like to see the sisters coming into all this because it is for them ; they belong to the race, designated ' *man*,' the kind of people that the revelation is for. " In him was life, and the life was the light of men," including women and children, whatever they are, they are all included in it. The sisters here to-day are here to learn and to get in the truth with the brothers and be like them as far as they may be according to divine directions.

J.K.P. Mr Darby's note to verse 2 refers to ' *such a one as that*.' Is that to emphasise His Person and that He was eternal ? Can you say anything more to help us in the matter of the control of our minds as giving them over to the contemplation of so great a Person ?

J.T. Well, I think the word *Logos* is what is in mind. Not anyone of us here perhaps knows much about Greek ; but it is clear that what we have been speaking of is clearing up our minds as to this question. When we sit down to the Lord's supper, we want our affections to be active, but the mind is active even there ; it is ' *for a calling of Me to mind*,' the Lord says. So that we should have our minds taken up with these things, and so should be able to speak accurately as to them.

J.S.Sr. Is that why the first operation was, " Let there be light " ?

J.T. Well, that is first, the idea of the day, that things are to be clear. And so in John's epistle, we are told that God is in the light, and that " if we walk in the light as *he* is in the light, we have fellowship one with another."

A.A.T. We have been talking about abstract

things, but is it not difficult for our minds to take in abstract things ?

J.T.   I do not think so, if we accustom our minds to it.   It is a question of how you have used your mind and how I have used mine.   Then we were talking just now about sisters, are they using their minds ?   Because God has given them minds too, and they are to be used.   It is very striking that the Lord's supper is said to be ' *for a calling of Me* to mind ' ; that is what the Lord said.   The same word is used as regards the bread *and* the cup.

E.P.   Is it your thought that the great teaching involved in these first three verses underlies all the teaching in this gospel ?

J.T.   That is right, those three wonderful verses.

THE PERSON OF CHRIST AND THE SPIRIT (2)

J.T. What is in mind now is to look into the matter of new birth. We are therefore treating of the operational side of the truth. We did not treat of that in our consideration of chapter 1, because we were speaking of the Person of the Lord Jesus as set before us there by the Spirit. There is no doubt that the Lord has been with us in this great matter, the greatest matter, we might say, that we could have before us. Now we are undertaking to look into what we may call the operations of the three Persons of the Godhead. The Spirit, specially is alluded to in the operation of new birth ; then the Father Himself, and the Son in verses 35 and 36, the Father having given all to be in the hands of the Son. " The Father loves the Son, and has given all things to be in his hand. He that believes on the Son has life eternal, and he that is not subject to the Son shall not see life, but the wrath of God abides upon him." In this section, as has been remarked, the subject in the main is eternal life, new birth leading up to it. Yet we have the idea of the Son of man being in heaven, so that we are still speaking of that line and the operational services rendered to us from there, but when we come to the real subject of eternal life, that is to say, formation brought forward in it, we have to see what comes down from heaven, the operations in relation to new birth and eternal life having to do with what is on the earth. This will require much inquiry and perhaps questioning, but what has been remarked I am sure is right, that new birth leading up to eternal life, and eternal life itself, have to do with the operations of the Spirit as here. When we come to chapter 7 it is the glorification of the Son of God so that the Spirit might come down formally, but that is not said here.

S.J.H. Does the thought of the wind blowing where it listeth give an indication of the sovereignty of a divine Person ?

J.T. Certainly, the sovereignty of the Spirit of God.

A.R. Does verse 2 of Genesis 1 suggest the idea of the operations of the Spirit ? It is said, that He hovered over the face of the deep.

J.T. Well, yes, hovering over the face of the deep, though there is not much there in the sense of operations. These are already stated in the fact that in the beginning God created the heavens and the earth, that is the great operational thought of God.

S.McC. Is there something in the fact that this matter of new birth comes up with a man that should have known better ? He was hindered intellectually in his apprehension of the truth, and therefore the necessity for emphasising the Spirit's sovereign action in the new birth.

J.T. Not only that, but he evidently was not a studious man, he was ignorant, really inexcusably ignorant, and I believe that has a great application at the present time. Why should we be ignorant when things are made so plain, and there is so much ministry, large volumes of the Collected Writings and all that ? They are available to us, why do we not read them ?

S.McC. The Lord referred to him as the teacher of Israel.

J.T. He was the teacher of Israel, and the Lord says, " thou . . . knowest not these things ? " He was ignorant really of the truth, he should have known the book of Ezekiel.

C.A.M. In that connection would you say that

the work of God had caused him at least to appreciate another teacher in coming to the Lord ?

J.T.   Yes, but it is a poor affair that he does not know more than he does.   We all are exposed to that sort of thing, we should know what is current, and we should not be saying things that are not right.   Not that I am saying a word against Nicodemus beyond what should be said, but he was not like Nathanael, who was a quick learner and did not miss anything ; the Lord credited him with it too.

W.S.   Luke in the opening of his gospel refers to himself, when he says, " it has seemed good to me also, accurately acquainted from the origin with all things."

J.T.   That is very good.   Now to get at the real point of the new birth here, is of first rate importance. Whether the brethren understand it or not is a question, because it is the Spirit's operation in a peculiar way.   It says that the wind blows where it will ; the wind is used as a figure, we have to understand that things are happening that are not always intelligible.   The Lord says, " thou canst not tell." That was not said of Nicodemus only, because in this matter nobody can tell ; it is the sovereign action of the Spirit.   You cannot just tell exactly what it means, but still it is there.

W.A.T.   Would that fit in with the thought you were expressing this morning of mystery ?   " Thou canst not tell."

J.T.   Well, it does.

S.McC.   The Lord said to Nicodemus, " Verily, verily, I say unto thee, we speak that which we know and we bear witness of that which we have seen, and ye receive not our witness."   The Lord is speaking in the dignity of His own intelligence, not as identified with the Jews.   There was a matter that had been laid before them, and the Lord says, You do not receive the witness.

J.T.   And I suppose the Lord means there, that He is not simply accusing Nicodemus, but the class that he represented, the Pharisees.   He belonged to a characteristic class, as it were.

S.McC.   The Lord introduces a class that does know.   He says, " We."

E.A.L.   We would like to hear more about the new birth.   Our natural birth is a birth which has an end in death, while new birth entering into eternal life has no end in death.

J.T.   That is good ;   only I would not link on what does not end in death so much with new birth. The full thought is eternal life, not new birth, if we are speaking of what does not end in death.

E.A.L.   I had in mind what the Lord said in John 17, " And this is the eternal life, that they should know thee, the only true God, and Jesus Christ whom thou hast sent."

J.T.   Well, that is a question of knowing, but there is more than merely knowing about what does not end in death.   That is in chapter 10.   The Lord says there, in speaking of the sheep, " My Father who has given them to me is greater than all, and no one can seize out of the hand of my Father."   That is the security we have as in the hands of the Father and the Son.   The idea conveyed in *new birth* is better expressed by " born anew," born *entirely afresh*, from the *top* really.   That is to say, an entirely different origin altogether, from natural birth.

A.N.W.   Judging by the meaning of that word *anew*, which the Lord used, its import should have prevented Nicodemus from making such a suggestion as that a man return to his mother's womb.   It is *born anew* from an entirely new source, it deals with the source as new entirely.

J.T.   Yes, therefore the subject is very clearly opened up.   " There was a man from among the Pharisees, his name Nicodemus, a ruler of the Jews ;

he came to him by night, and said to him, Rabbi, we know that thou art come a teacher from God, for none can do these signs that thou doest unless God be with him." Well, that is so far so good, but then the Lord says to him, " Verily, verily," an expression which occurs about twenty-four times in John's gospel. " Verily, verily, I say unto thee, Except any one," not simply a man, but any one ; " Except any one be born anew he cannot see the kingdom of God." The point the Lord is making is what a man can see, and then what a man can enter into, whether he can see the kingdom of God, and whether he can enter into it. That is what I feel should guide our minds now ; it is a question of the kingdom of God and what the operations here have in mind in that relation.

Ques. Was Nicodemus a subject of new birth ?

J.T. What he said was very vague, and shallow. Even in chapter 19 his part is not very brilliant. He and Joseph of Arimathæa are linked together there. Then in chapter 7 he said a word of defence for the Lord, but at the same time there is a lack in him. Over against him Nathanael learned quickly, he took things up and learned them quickly. We should not be ever learning and never coming to the knowledge of the truth.

J.H.P. Would you say a word as to the expression, " Except anyone be born anew, he cannot see the kingdom of God " ?

J.T. Why does the Lord allude to that ? It is a question of the moral sway of God in these circumstances ; that God has to say to all these matters. You must listen to what He has to say ; I think that is what is meant without going into it too much. The Lord just touches on it, as if He would say, ' Nicodemus, you need to see the kingdom of God, and you need to enter into the kingdom of God too.' I think the Lord meant that he really was a subject of the work of God, but a very poor one, a very poor learner ; and we might say, that we are all in that class, very poor learners.

V.C.L. Would it be in your mind, that with the place the Spirit is gaining in our hearts this matter of new birth and seeing and entering the kingdom should be much clearer than it has been before ?

J.T. I would say that ; much clearer, because we are very hazy ; not that I want to be critical of the dear brethren, because I am including myself ; we are very hazy about things, and yet there is wonderful instruction available to us. It is remarkable the amount of ministry that the Lord is giving and has been giving all through these times of the revival up till now. There is a great need of those who can lead, who know what to do and what to say, great need everywhere, so that the brethren should not be hazy about things.

Rem. Paul says to Timothy, " Think of what I say, for the Lord will give thee understanding in all things."

J.T. Just so, " the Lord will give thee understanding." We are to think on these things, we are to consider them and to consider the ministers, as to whether they are able to say what is right.

V.C.L. Is there any point in the fact that Nicodemus is referring to the Lord's own signs, and the Lord immediately turns his mind to the Spirit's operations ?

J.T. Well, the Lord opened up the whole matter, a wonderful opening up of things in relation to the sovereign action of the Spirit ; that is what this chapter is. The Lord said to Nicodemus, " The wind blows where it will, and thou hearest its voice, but knowest not whence it comes and where it goes : thus is everyone that is born of the Spirit." Now there are references to three matters ; being born of the Spirit and then seeing and entering into the

27

kingdom of God. Then, " Nicodemus answered and
said to him, " How can these things be ? " He was
alluding to nature of course. Jesus answered and
said to him, " *Thou* " ; the thou is emphatic, " Thou
art the teacher of Israel and knowest not these
things ! Verily, verily, I say unto thee, We speak
that which we know, and we bear witness of that
which we have seen, and ye receive not our witness.
If I have said the earthly things to you, and ye
believe not, how, if I say the heavenly things to
you, will ye believe ? " The Lord here is not dealing
only with Nicodemus, He is dealing with his class,
the kind of people he is linked with. Now, Nicodemus
must think over this matter of heavenly things, and
consider what it means, and we can very well do the
same. Then in verse 13, " And no one has gone up
into heaven, save he who came down out of heaven,
the Son of man who is in heaven. And as Moses
lifted up the serpent in the wilderness, thus must
the Son of man be lifted up, that everyone who
believes on him may not perish, but have life eternal."
So that God has reached His great point in eternal
life already, in this verse. At the same time it is a
question of the Son of man going up into heaven, and
being in heaven, and what could Nicodemus say
about that ? What can we say about it, because it
is a mysterious thing, it is a mystery, that the Lord
should be in heaven as the Son of man, and yet
He is here on earth.

S.J.H. Would not the fact that the wind has
blown our way accelerate our ability to learn more
quickly ? These wonderful things as to the Holy
Spirit and the current ministry, have come our way,
and they are really ours. The wind blows where it
will, and many have not heard it apparently, but we
have, and one delights in it, that it is a sovereign
matter of the Spirit of God.

J.T. Now we have to just touch on things and

move on. It says, " And no one has gone up into heaven, save he who came down out of heaven, the Son of man who is in heaven." That is a mysterious thing that the Lord could say that of Himself. We have to understand that there is mystery attached to His Person. He could say that He was the Son of man in heaven and yet He was here on earth, talking to Nicodemus.

S.McC. In that connection it has been said questioningly sometimes in regard to this matter of addressing the Spirit, How can we address the Spirit, a Person within us ? Is that not putting limits on a divine Person ? We cannot limit Him to just what He is as in us.

J.T. Just so ; and so when the Lord was here, you could not speak of Him or to Him as you would speak to an ordinary man, because you could not fathom what was there. The same is true now, the presence of the Spirit of God is unfathomable, we cannot understand it. People around us do not understand what we are talking about, they are outside of it ; but we have light and I am sure that the Lord is pleased to see us here this afternoon and all interested.

A.R. The Spirit of God is here objectively and subjectively at the same time, is He not ?

J.T. Well, quite so ; He can be viewed objectively as you can speak of anybody objectively at a distance from you. You can apprehend Him and speak of Him in that objective way.

R.P. Would you say something as to " that which is born of the Spirit is spirit " ?

J.T. It would show that there is a wonderful character of operations going on here on earth just now. Presently it will cease when the dispensation ceases, but there is something going on in the assembly now that we can name as of the Spirit, of which we can say that it is *spirit*. " That which is born of the flesh is flesh; and that which is born of the Spirit is spirit." We can name it. We might say that the word *spirit* applies to nearly everybody in this room.

F.N.W. In the preceding chapter the Lord did not trust Himself to them; but does this matter of *spirit*, " that which is born of the Spirit is spirit," establish a trustworthy base upon which these other things can be built ?

J.T. The Lord could not trust them, because the idea of spirit was not there; there was just ignorance as to all that was going on, but Nicodemus was not like that, there was something in him that the Lord could address as spirit. I believe He appreciated Nicodemus in that sense. So that he is seen again in chapter 7, and he goes right through to chapter 19.

F.C. Do you think he was hindered because he was not ready to leave the Sanhedrim, he was not ready to leave his religious position ?

J.T. Just so, but still there was something in him. He represents a class of people who are not against us or the truth; indeed there is something in them that indicates that God is working with them, and we have to be very patient with them, so that they may come to light at last. Nicodemus did come into the light at last, in chapter 19.

A.B. Elisha asks for a double portion of Elijah's spirit. I wondered whether that would bear on what has been said about the Spirit being within us and alongside of us ?

J.T. Elisha wanted to get a good supply of the spirit of Elijah, and Elijah said, " If thou see me when I am taken from thee, it shall be so to thee." You have to be alert to get this.

Ques. The Lord speaks first of seeing, then of entering into the kingdom of God. Would that suggest movement in intelligence ?

J.T. Seeing is of course an action of the eye, and

entering is an action of the mind. Unless one is born anew he has no sight at all, he does not see anything. But then he must be born of water and of Spirit to enter into the kingdom of God. There are the two things, water and Spirit. Born of water is a sort of negative or cleansing idea and the Spirit is a positive idea, meaning that new birth has taken place and there is the sense of being in spirit, as the Lord says, " that which is born of the Spirit is spirit." That is what we want to get at, whether we are all in this concrete thing here to-day. It is the idea of the spirit given to this one and that one. Perhaps everybody here to-day has the Spirit, but if not he may be born anew. We are therefore dealing with positive things this afternoon.

McC. Does " That which is born of the Spirit is spirit," involve a change of heart ? I was thinking of your allusion to Ezekiel 36.

J.T. The word there is " I will give you a new heart." It is to that the Lord alludes when He says to Nicodemus, " Thou art the teacher of Israel and knowest not these things ! " Nicodemus ought to have known these things.

G.W. Do you think Nathanael as having come from Cana of Galilee would be characterised by having witnessed the glory the Lord had displayed in that place ? It says at the end of the gospel that Nathanael was of Cana and that is where the Lord manifested His glory. I am endeavouring to link it on with what you said about Nathanael as a quick learner, and connecting it with the glory and the Spirit's operations.

J.T. Nathanael became an apostle, you know, he became an apostle in the Lord's ministry, he became quite a distinguished man, but Nicodemus did not. The need for those who lead is very great. Nathanael began to lead ; he was one of the seven that went with Peter going to fish, but he became a useful man afterwards. The Lord said to Nicodemus, " We speak that which we know," and the point is that we should get to know things and convey them to others, because there is so much need of teaching.

J.H.P. Is there the thought of each divine Person operating sovereignly in this chapter ? First the Spirit, as typified in the wind, and then in verse 13, " he who came down out of heaven," and then in verse 16, " For God so loved the world, that he gave his only-begotten Son." Is there a progressive suggestion in that way ?

J.T. That is right. The three divine Persons are seen operating here. We are dealing with the operational side now, and the point is that eternal life comes into view. The Lord Himself speaks of it, but He says, *God* ; that " God so loved the world." In saying that, He is speaking about eternal life.

Ques. What is the difference between being born of the Spirit, and the Spirit coming upon them in Acts 19 ?

J.T. The Spirit coming upon us is when we get sealed. It is when you get the Spirit that the Spirit comes upon you. Nicodemus had not got thus far clearly.

W.A.T. Would you preach about being born of the Spirit in the gospel ?

J.T. I would say that in some sense you must. I would put it to people who were listening to the truth, You must see to it that you are born anew. It is a good question to raise with people, are they born again ? But with that you want to be sure they have the Spirit too ; you want to raise the question, Are you sealed with the Spirit ?

W.A.T. Paul says, in Acts 19, " Did ye receive the Holy Spirit ? "

J.T. Just so, and they said they did not know the Spirit was there at all, they did not know the Spirit was being given.

J.H.P. Is it significant that the reference to life eternal comes after all three divine Persons have been referred to as operating ?

J.T. I think on the whole that it is the objective presentation of the subject of eternal life in this section. When we come to chapter 6 we get the subjective side of things, because it is a question of what comes down from heaven ; " the bread of God is he who comes down out of heaven." Here we have the actual operations of the three Persons in the objective sense. We have to go to chapter 6 to get the real thought of eternal life as down here in the sense of the bread of God coming down from heaven.

S.M. The question of believing enters in here, does it not ? " He that believes."

J.T. Yes. The principle running through John's gospel is faith. " How is it that ye do not believe ? " the Lord says. We are so prone to be just literal in our conversations, and remarks, and questions.

L.L.P. Would the point of believing be stressed, by the fact that in the passage read there is a penalty for unbelief ?

J.T. In verses 35 and 36, you mean. " The Father loves the Son, and has given all things to be in his hand. He that believes on the Son has life eternal, and he that is not subject to the Son shall not see life, but the wrath of God abides upon him." It is a terrible thing that comes out there, and it is in connection with things being given into the hands of the Son by the Father. This question comes up, that a man may not be subject to the Son and hence not have eternal life at all, and in that case the wrath of God abides on him, one of the most solemn things in the whole book.

V.C.L. Is it right to say that those who are born again shall surely receive the Holy Spirit from the

Father, because of this being the Spirit's dispensation ?

J.T. Quite so. Some say, that there will be people who are the subjects of the work of God in the present period, who will not get the Spirit at all, and will not come into the assembly. I do not think that is so. While the Spirit is here every person who is the subject of the work of God will come into the assembly. It is a very comforting thought.

JOHN 4 : 1–30

J.T.   We finished yesterday with an allusion to
verses 35 and 36 of chapter 3, and there can be no
doubt that chapter 4 opens up the position of the
Son's appointment to all things as set forth there.
Here the feminine side of humanity comes into view,
so that we have to consider how the feminine side is
worked out in relation to eternal life and also in
relation to the service of God.   The operational side
is, of course, in view still, and will be throughout,
the subjects being taken up in perfect order.   Now
speaking of the feminine side, we have had it already
in chapter 2, but it is taken up here clearly in relation
to the vessel.   The Lord is seen here as having all
things given into His hands, as it says, in chapter 3,
" The Father loves the Son, and has given all things
to be in his hand.   He that believes on the Son has
life eternal, and he that is not subject to the Son
shall not see life, but the wrath of God abides upon
him."   So that now the Person who is the great
Operator in the economy is before us, and that is the
Son.   The mind travels to Genesis 1 in view of all
that has happened, and the area in which the happen-
ings occurred ; that is, the expanse ; the immense
expanse that God has opened up as the sphere of
His operations.   The Operator there was God ; as
it says, " In the beginning God created the heavens
and the earth."   Now He has an appointed One in
the Son, the Son is the Operator now, and the Father
loves Him.

F.N.W.   Has He that unique place as being in the
bosom of the Father ?

J.T.   That is what you get in chapter 1, and
chapter 3 says, " The Father loves the Son."

A.N.W. Then coming out into operation the Spirit elects to call Him Lord. The chapter opens with the title " *Lord*," which is quite unusual. " When therefore the Lord knew."

Ques. Is this woman material for the operations ?

J.T. Exactly ; she is an example of the material and how it is formed, and then she begins to operate herself, she moves herself. So that *the Lord* is seen here as administrating. We may use the word *administration* as well as operation in connection with the term *Lord*.

F.N.W. " My Father worketh hitherto and I work," what is involved in that ?

J.T. That is chapter 5 which we shall not touch by itself. The allusion is to the fact that the Father had been operating from the first of Genesis, but that the Son is now operating. That chapter opens up how the Father and Son are operating together, but here the Son is operating by Himself as appointed, as being the Administrator, the One whom the Father loves ; a very precious thought.

S.McC. Would the fact that a woman comes into view in chapter 4 immediately following this formal statement of the economy in the end of chapter 3, suggest in principle that one of the prime thoughts in the operations of the economy is the assembly ?

J.T. Quite so. Hence the thought runs through the book in certain women, culminating in Mary Magdalene, the one who recognises that the Lord is her Teacher. So the Lord proceeds here carefully, because it is a careful operation. The Lord pursues the subject until He comes to the matter of her husband. " Go, call thy husband." Of course the wife normally should be at the call of her husband, but in this case the husband is at the call of the wife. That is a thing to be noticed by wives and husbands, as to how we move together in the economy.

W.A.T. In chapter 3 : 36, where it speaks of

being subject to the Son, Mr. Darby says, ' It is the obedience of submission to His Person.' Would that feature be set out in this woman ?

J.T. I think so ; it is a subject that runs through the gospel. The Son is seen there as loved by the Father, and anyone who is not subject to the Son is subject to eternal judgment.

J.S.Sr. Are the Son's movements to be noted here ? " He must needs go through Samaria."

J.T. You mean the Lord's movements. That *need* would undoubtedly bear on the fact that this woman comes into evidence, because it is a question of the material that the Lord had in mind to bring about for the assembly.

S.M. Does it magnify the operations, in that the branches run over the wall ?

J.T. Very good, that is from Genesis 49. Joseph's branches run over the wall. In the woman's mind the wall stood between the Samaritans and the Jews, but then the Lord as the true Joseph is here and the branches run over the wall.

Ques. As this conversation goes on, there is exposure brought about in this woman ; I suppose making room for the work of God ?

J.T. It was to clear out the dross. The Lord works to clear out dross wherever it is, and the dross is everywhere ; but then the service of the Lord is to clear it away, and she gives evidence of clearance by leaving her waterpot and going her way into the city to the men, showing that she was not afraid of them now morally ; she could evangelise them. Before this it would have been quite different ; for she had had five husbands.

E.P. Was this woman previously a subject of the work of the Spirit ?

J.T. I do not think she is so seen ; she is just in her natural state. She is a Samaritan and the Lord a Jew, but she is not long in being adjusted and that brings out this wonderful material, that a woman should leave her waterpot and go her way into the city and come to the men, and say, " Come, see a man who told me all things I had ever done : is not he the Christ ? " The fact that He could tell her everything that she had ever done was the evidence of it ; He is the Christ.

J.K. Is there any thought in her coming to draw water, that she feels her need ?

J.T. Well, she is in need, but it is just a natural need such as you might find with anybody, and the Lord was pleased to open a conversation with her. It says, " And he must needs pass through Samaria. He comes therefore to a city of Samaria called Sychar, near to the land which Jacob gave to his son Joseph." That is the historical position, and of course history has a great deal to do with the testimony. This matter extends back to the days of Jacob, when Jacob gave something to his son Joseph. But who is the Son now, and who is Jacob now ? It is God, and the Son is Christ, and the material to be operated upon is the woman, just an ordinary woman, but a woman who has had five husbands, and therefore a very poor affair, a poor corrupt affair ; yet the Lord is undertaking to make her material for the assembly. Following on this, we get a Mary Magdalene in chapter 20.

H.B. Would you say that Jesus sitting "*as he was*" stands in contrast to all that was seen in the woman ?

J.T. That is true, He does not make any show, He does not make any pretence at all, He is just as He was, a tired Man. Fancy that, the Lord of glory, just a tired Man in the service of God.

J.K.P. Notwithstanding what enters into the history of this woman, does this chapter stand out in contrast to chapter 3, showing how the work of God comes forward rapidly in this person ?

J.T. It is the converse of chapter 3 really, because

it is the subjective side, whereas chapter 3 is the objective side, the Father's work; the Father's work in love. It is a question there of the love of God, not the love of Christ exactly, or the love of the Spirit, but the love of God, " God *so* loved " ; that is chapter 3 ; it is the great objective thought in God. The difficulty with this woman was serious indeed, but the Lord bottomed the thing quickly, and brought out the greatest matter as a result ; namely, the worship of God. So that we may look for the greatest things where difficulties arise, because God has great things in His mind for us and He wants us to be ready for them. This woman was the material ready for what God is doing, and she is yielding, undoubtedly under the guiding hand of the Spirit. She brings up the question of worship, a very unlikely subject for her, to speak of, but the Lord does not say a word against it. He only says, " Go, call thy husband," as much as to say, this matter is so great your husband should be in it ; what you are doing, he should be doing, otherwise there is something wrong.

L.L.P. Would the scripture " where sin abounded grace has overabounded," be fulfilled in her case ?

J.T. Well, sin abounded in this woman as it does in everybody really, " for all have sinned, and come short of the glory of God." However sin abounded particularly with her, the Lord knew it, and He proceeded to undo everything. He was here to undo the works of the devil.

A.R. The woman says, " Sir, I see that thou art a prophet," showing how quickly she learned.

J.T. The thought of prophetic ministry came before us specially about twenty-five years ago and God has greatly blessed it. It was of God that the saints should take up the idea of prophetic ministry and have meetings for that purpose ; they have been greatly blessed of God ; they bring out the action of God, the divine action in prophetic service, because God would work on prophetic lines. There is so much to be known, even future events entering into it.

A.A.T. Why does the Lord introduce the thought of eternal life with her ?

J.T. Because that is the main subject in John, and He returns to it when the time comes for it ? But then she had introduced the question of divine service, a matter that an ordinary woman would not bring up. He does not say, You should not speak of that ; He takes her on at once. The Father, He says, seeks worshippers. She had talked about worship, but the Lord says, The Father seeks worshippers, and He seeks them to worship Him in spirit and in truth.

V.C.L. Would you say a word as to why in this section which is the sphere of the Son's operations, we get the word *water*, or an allied term used about twenty-four times in the verses read ? Is there something significant for us to understand as to the freedom of the Spirit where the Son is made way for ?

J.T. Very good. John has his own way of emphasising things and we do well to observe them, as with this question of water. Now it says, in verse 6, " It was about the sixth hour. A woman comes out of Samaria to draw water. Jesus says to her, Give me to drink," as much as to say, I am in need too, I am in need of water ; You give Me to drink. But then it says further, " for his disciples had gone away into the city that they might buy provisions." Why did they all go ? Why should they all need to go to buy provisions ? Well, they did and left Him alone, a most extraordinary thing. " The Samaritan woman therefore says to him, How dost thou, being a Jew, ask to drink of me who am a Samaritan, for Jews have no intercourse with Samaritans," as if the Lord did not know. " Jesus answered and said to her, If thou knewest the gift

of God." Do you know anything about that ?
That is in effect what the Lord says. She had seemed
to know everything so far ; she knew about the
difference between the Samaritans and the Jews,
but then the Lord says, " If thou knewest the gift
of God," do you know anything about that ? that
is the next thing.

G.H. Would that bring out the Lord's skilfulness
in the way He approached the woman ? " Give me
to drink."

J.T. That is right.

Ques. Is there anything in the fact that Abraham's
servant approached Rebecca similarly ?

J.T. In Genesis 24, you mean. That brings up
the whole burning subject, because that man,
Abraham's servant, was a type of the Spirit of God
Himself. Abraham's servant was very particular as
to what he should do about this matter of water.

W.A.T. Would you say that it is the desire of all
three divine Persons, at the present time especially
to be refreshed in this way, the Father, the Son, and
the Holy Spirit ?

J.T. That is right.

A.N.W. It is striking that in view of His asking
for a drink the Lord should say, " the Father seeketh."
The economy seems to bring all three Persons into it.

J.T. So the Lord says, " If thou knewest the
gift of God " ; a marvellous thing ! It is said in
Romans to be eternal life ; " the gift of God is
eternal life."

E.A.L. This woman does not seem to be personal-
ised in this chapter at all. There seem to be thirteen
mentions of *woman* ; the Lord uses it just once,
after she confessed that He was a prophet. The other
references to His speaking to her are all impersonal.
Would you help us in that ?

J.T. You mean it is impersonal because her name
is not mentioned ? But the word *woman* is the point.

The Lord used it in addressing His mother in chapter 2. He used the very same word, *woman*. It is a very noble word, it is next to man.

E.A.L. He does not call her *woman* until she confesses that He is a prophet.

J.T. Just so, then He recognises her as a woman, a very noble word that she is entitled to. Of course, the whole matter the Lord is working out hinges on the fact that she is a woman.

E.A.L. When the men of the city return they speak of her as *the* woman ; they heard her confess the Lord, they got help through her.

J.T. She was completely changed. She left her waterpot, giving up her calling altogether, and going out to the men. Well, now, the Lord says, You can be used. He had already said, I am the Christ. He says to her, so to speak, You say, When the Christ comes He will tell us all things, but I am He ! " I who speak to thee am he." Wonderful ! It is a question of operations, the Christ as the great Operator of God, *the* Christ, and she is coming to that, she is coming into His operations.

J.VanS. Is that what the Lord had in mind in saying, " If thou knewest the gift of God " ? He at once refers to who He is, and then to what He would be able to give, living water.

J.T. Did she know it, though ? " If thou knewest the gift of God, and who it is." It is marvellous that He should bring that in ! The greatest things are brought in, and she has to do with them.

J.H.P. Is it significant that these remarks as to the refreshment of a divine Person are addressed to a woman ?

J.T. It is marvellous that He does not object to her bringing up the matter of worship, though to answer it the whole moral question must be brought up. Persons go to places with a steeple on them, that they call places of worship, yet they have no right on moral lines to have any part in the worship of God.

R.P. I would like some help on the feminine side of the service of God.

J.T. In result, the feminine side is represented in all Christians, in all the saints, and the masculine side is represented in Christ alone. In full result that is the position, " His wife has made herself ready," and it is man and woman ; the Man is Christ and the woman is the assembly. That is what is in the mind of God, and in the Lord's mind in this chapter. The feminine side is in the saints who form the assembly, and the masculine side is in Himself as Man, " For God is one, and the Mediator of God and man one, the man Christ Jesus," 1 Tim. 2 : 5.

Ques. Going back to God's operations in Genesis, woman became the counterpart of man, so in that way the assembly is the counterpart of Christ, would you say ?

J.T. Quite so ; that is what the Lord is aiming at here. But that is especially Paul's line, while John is operating in connection with it, bringing out the kind of material that forms it. That is what John has in his mind ; so that we have Mary Magdalene in chapter 20, and the Samaritan woman here, and the Lord's own mother in chapter 2 ; and several others too, including Mary of Bethany, in this most wonderful book.

S.McC. Had you anything special in mind in connection with the bearing of eternal life on the feminine side ?

J.T. I think it is just what comes out here, that it is a question of *living* water, what He would give. She could give an ordinary drink of water, but what could He give ! " If thou knewest the gift of God and who it is that says to thee, Give me to drink, thou wouldest have asked of him and he would have given thee *living* water." That is the great point to have in mind. This matter of living water comes up in the book of Revelation. Here the water springs up, but in chapter 6 we shall see the idea of eternal life in the sustenance of it, is in the bread that comes down. It comes down from heaven, and the bread is Christ.

A.N.W. Is that not the point in John 3 ? I think you were saying that it is His being given in John 3 : 16, but the water springs up and it is on the feminine subjective side in John 4.

J.T. That is right. It springs up here.

S.J.H. Why is the word *become* put in verse 14 ? " Shall become in him."

J.T. It suggests the possibility of change. John the evangelist says, " I became in the Spirit " ; and it is said of the Lord Jesus in chapter 1 that the Word became flesh, showing the possibility of change. So here the water changes, it becomes *a fountain*. " The water which I shall give him shall become in him a fountain of water springing up into eternal life." There is some marvellous mysterious effect brought about in that something becomes something different in a person. The water springs up into eternal life, showing that here the great thought of eternal life has an upward movement ; but in chapter 6 it is not an upward movement but a downward movement, the Son of man came down from heaven and gives His life, His flesh for the life of the world.

J.K.P. These operations seem to commence with the idea of the sixth hour ; and then the Lord goes on to mention that " the hour is coming and now is." Is that linked on with the urgency of coming into what is current in the Spirit's operations at this present time ?

J.T. Just so. We were talking of geography in verse 5, but this is a matter of time. The question of time and the question of geography both come into this chapter, and all that is of great importance.

E.P.   Would you say that eternal life as presented here is essential and basic to the enjoyment of the full Christian position ?

J.T.   It is basic just as new birth is basic to eternal life.   Here eternal life is basic to the true Christian position and basic to the service of God.

McC.   We must have the Spirit to enjoy eternal life.

J.T.   I would certainly say that.   The water here is the Spirit, and it becomes a fountain ; it is springing up into everlasting life.

W.A.T.   May I ask a little more about the matter of refreshment ?   The sixth hour was mentioned just now, which was the hour that the Lord entered upon the darkness that came upon the whole land. It was just at this hour that the Lord says to the woman, " Give me to drink."   Is there some connection, would you say ?

J.T.   There must be.   You are talking about the Lord's death and it is a question of time as we were saying, and of how God uses time. He made it, and He was the first to use it.   And so the Lord's supper came in in time, on the first day of the week when the disciples came together to break bread.   With anyone wanting to break bread to-day, the moral question must come up, as to whether she or he is fit to break bread.   The Lord brought it up with this woman.

V.C.L.   The woman says, " Sir, I see that thou art a prophet."   Would that indicate that she has been born anew and therefore sees the kingdom of God ?   And then when she says at the end, " Is not he the Christ ? " would that suggest that she has been born of water and of spirit and has entered the kingdom ?

J.T.   Well, you might say that.

W.A.T. You were speaking just now in connection with persons being fit to break bread. As we know, no one should break bread who has not the Spirit. How would you detect that a person has the Spirit, especially with young children ?

J.T. First of all, I would say, do they like to be with the older brethren, or do they congregate by themselves, which is a baneful thing for children. I would say if they want to be with the older brethren, that is a good sign that they are fit to break bread ; but if they associate only with the younger people it would be questionable, because they ought to know that the older brethren are likely to have the truth. It is not good to see young people flocking together and ignoring the older brothers and sisters.

W.A.T. I think that is very helpful, and one would especially look for it during special meetings such as these, that the young people should keep with the older brethren.

J.T. I would say that. It is a baneful thing to see them flocking together, nothing good comes out of it, laughing and talking, that is all, whereas they ought to keep with the older brethren.

B.W. We had the thought last night of discernment. Would that be seen in this woman that she discerned that the Lord was a prophet ? And she discerned that she should leave her waterpot.

J.T. Very good, like Abigail. David said to her " Blessed be thy discernment." Abigail was a discerner. She was a type of the assembly.

A. Macd. Would you say that discernment was seen in Rebecca too ? She said, " Drink, my lord," she discerned who was there.

J.T. Exactly, and she said, I will give your camels drink too, a great idea. Think of a girl like that ready to water ten camels, how much water they would drink. But then we are in John 4, and the

point here is that the Lord has the water. The
woman has ordinary water and has a water vessel
to carry it, but she left that behind her. The Lord
had living water, and He calls it " the water that *I*
shall give him," because the Giver is the Lord Himself.
Who can define what that water is ? because it
changes by some action of the Lord's when it enters
into the person of the believer. It becomes in him
a fountain of water springing up into everlasting life.
That is a mysterious thing, and that happens in
all of us.

E.A.L.   You have helped us to see that we cannot
limit the scope of the types, as in Genesis 24 and the
types of the Spirit there. Things change and
develop, do they not ?

J.T.   Quite so. The question of wells comes in
that chapter too, because Isaac was coming and
going from the well Beer-lahai-roi. He was coming
and going, as if he had plenty of leisure for Rebecca
when she was coming to him. That suggests a wonderful matter ; it needs leisure for that. If we are thinking of Christ as Head of the assembly, well, He has
leisure for that, He is ready for us. The Lord says, I
have time, I am coming and going from the well.
It was that particular well at which Sarah's servant
was found. She got benefit from that well, and the
Lord is figuratively seen there, and here comes
Rebecca. Well, that is wonderful ! The Lord is
ready for her.

S.M.   David's mighty men broke through when
David longed for a drink.

J.T.   Quite so. They discerned the longing of
David's heart. He was once a boy at that place—
at Hebron, and they discerned his longings and broke
through and got the drink, but he poured it out for
a drink offering.

Ques. It says that this water springs up into
everlasting life. That would be in the renewed

47

man, would it not ? It would not spring up in everybody.

J.T. It springs up in a meeting like this. Those of us who have come together form an area in which the Spirit of God can operate, and He is doing it at this present time. He is springing up, morally, in our minds.

W.P. This fountain is not only for our enjoyment, but for God's enjoyment, is it not ?

J.T. Indeed it is. God is working out everything for His own pleasure and His thoughts are to be consummated in the seventh day of the creation ; that is to say, the millennium. That is God's day. God is going to have a wonderful time in the millennium.

W.W. And that is why the thought is brought in that God is seeking worshippers ?

J.T. Exactly. The Lord says, " God is a spirit." He never said that to anybody before. In chapter 1, the word says, " no one has seen God at any time." Now the Lord says here, that " God is a spirit," and that the Father is seeking those who can worship Him in spirit and in truth. Are we among these worshippers ? Are we all in the area of everlasting life. Because it is to be known right here on the earth where the brethren are together. We may have wonderful times, even touching what is in heaven.

A.R. It says, " the Father seeketh . . . worshippers," but it does not say, God seeks them. It says, " God is a spirit, and they who worship him must worship him in spirit and in truth." There is a difference, is there not ?

J.T. It says, " the Father seeks *such* as his worshippers." The *such* ; who are they ? What are these people ? They are persons who worship in spirit and in truth. That is to say, it is your spirit, your own spirit, but then there is truth attached to it. You have the Spirit, but then you must have the idea of truth. The Father seeks worshippers on those lines.

J.S.Sr. The *such* applies to living persons, does it not ?

J.T. It does, indeed. You add the idea of persons or vessels.

A.A.T. Does the Father have the first place in the economy ?

J.T. Oh, surely. That is the order, you could not reverse the order. When you are baptising a person you could not reverse the order of Matthew 28. The order is the name of the Father, and of the Son, and of the Spirit ; you could not reverse that order and say the name of the Spirit, and of the Son, and of the Father. Morally it must be done that way.

A.R. Does *God* in this chapter include the three Persons in the Godhead ?

J.T. I think so. It says, " God is a spirit," that includes the three Persons.

A.R. The One who is seeking worshippers is the Father.

J.T. The Father is specified, but then it does not say, the Father is a spirit, it says, " God is a spirit." " The Father seeks such as his worshippers."

Ques. " But the hour is coming and now is, when the true worshippers shall worship the Father." What time is that ?

J.T. Now. It is the present time. It has been so far approximately two thousand years. The time will cease presently, but the *now* is the present time ; that is to say, we are in it, a wonderful time.

A.R. The fact that we worship *God* as God, which includes the three divine Persons ought to help us in regard to worshipping the Spirit by Himself, do you think ?

J.T. Yes.

B.W. So that the truth regarding the Spirit would enhance the service of God, would it not ?

J.T. It would. The expression " in spirit and in truth," refers to your own spirit ; that is to say, you are spiritual, and you are characterised by the truth.

A.N.W. In contrast to the materialistic worship around and the false religion of Samaria.

J.T. Yes, the spiritualistic materialism that enters into man's worship.

A.D. Would you help us as to " we have both access by one Spirit to the Father " ?

J.T. The access, the instrumentality of the access is Christ Himself, it is " through him." But the movement is by the Spirit ; for " through him we have both access by one Spirit to the Father." The word *both* refers to Jew and Gentile, as if God intended that there should be both Jew and Gentile in the assembly.

THE PERSON OF CHRIST AND THE SPIRIT (4)

JOHN 6 : 27–58 ; 66–71

J.T. The last verses read are suggested because they bear so much as to their teaching on the whole chapter, and they are intended to appeal to us here and now as to whether we hold on to the truth or leave it. " From that time," it says, " many of his disciples went away back and walked no more with him. Jesus therefore said to the twelve, Will ye also go away ? " Peter's reply is, " Lord, to whom shall we go ? thou hast words of life eternal." So it is in regard to this appeal that these final verses are read, because they should come home to us as to continuance in the truth. They are addressed to the twelve, and Judas is in mind as the traitor, showing how we are to be challenged by the truth in this sense. It is a very long chapter, 71 verses, but the words of eternal life govern the whole chapter.

J.S.Sr. This side is the eating rather than drinking, is it not ?

J.T. Yes, the idea too of the bread of life, coming down.

S.McC. In the course of these meetings you have stressed more than once the thought of eternal life in John 6 as connected with what comes down. Would you open out a little more what is on your mind in connection with the coming down ?

J.T. I think it ought to be borne in mind that eternal life in the main is for the earth. It is linked up with heaven, of course, hence the fourth chapter makes much of the water of life springing up, so that we have to keep the two thoughts in mind so as to have right balance. Eternal life is really here where death is, but at the same time there is the power to raise us up, however long we may have to wait. The last day will see it consummated ; that we are to be raised up. The bread of life is to maintain us in life here where the testimony is, hence the first verse that we read ; " Work not for the food which perishes, but for the food which abides unto life eternal, which the Son of man shall give to you ; for him has the Father sealed, even God." It is a question of food or sustenance where the testimony is, and we are not to be making the natural every-thing, but what abides unto life eternal.

C.A.M. I was wondering whether it would be right to connect the thought of the springing up, in chapter 4, with the words *abide* and *dwell*, that so constantly occur in this passage ; as to whether we reach a sort of objective in that way as to eternal life ?

J.T. Just so, it abides, it goes through, because the millennial world will be a world of men as we are in flesh and blood, but then there has to be some change in order to condition us for eternity ; and therefore the idea of continuance and of abiding, that death will not overtake us as a penalty, that we are to be raised up. There is a certainty as to it, we are to be raised up at the last day.

A.N.W. The Lord speaks of the Spirit in the chapter as quickening, " It is the Spirit which quickens." He has to say, " the flesh profits nothing." Would you say where the Spirit comes in in this matter ? Is it that He comes into every apprehension we may have of this and every other feature of the truth ?

J.T. The question therefore is whether the Lord Jesus Himself comes alone for us to change us, or whether the Spirit has a part in it too, and we may say, both are true. Romans 8 would say that the Spirit quickens, so that He too has a part in it.

A.N.W. " Shall quicken your mortal bodies," you mean.

J.T.   Yes. Quickening our mortal bodies because
of the Spirit which dwells in us. That would, of
course, solve the question of eternity, and when we
say eternity we must include eternal life ; though
eternal life in itself is more limited in thought.
It has a peculiar application to the millennial day
in that God has a way of keeping men and women
and children alive on this earth in that day. There
will be ultimately new heavens and a new earth,
" wherein dwells righteousness," according to 2
Peter, and he says, we await that. But in the
meantime God will have His way as to things.
The course of time evidently is divided up into
seven periods, and we are coming on to the seventh
day which is, I think, the millennial day. We are
living within the period of testimony, the assembly
has part in that. But in the last day God will raise
us up ; we come into that according to the promise ;
we come into the idea of being raised up even if we
have to wait for the last day. At the same time
there will be a life here on earth in the millennial
day in which God will have His way and show that
He can keep men alive on the earth without dying.
I do not believe the millennium will be marked by
death at all, although a man may live one hundred
years and yet die, but in general the idea in the
millennium is eternal life.

S.McC.   As to the millennium, do you regard it
as quickly coming, or will there be a gradual development or change in things ?

J.T.   If we look at the prophetic side, I believe
there will be a gradual change. But we have a
complete idea as to the thing. The Lord Himself
will not be here until the falling away happens,
and I believe that will happen as soon as the assembly
is taken to heaven. But then God will carry on His
earthly thoughts as to Israel, His final thoughts,
so that all Israel shall be saved ; all Israel, meaning

the whole twelve tribes. The whole divine ideal will be realised in the millennial day. It will be a wonderful day, marked out to show the devil and his upholders what God can do in spite of conditions. He can in general abolish death and keep men and women and children alive on the earth, because children are alluded to in the millennial day, and old men and old women too. The Lord is saying here that the Father will draw all that shall come to Him ; the Father therefore will act in relation to the Lord. There will be a means of dealing with death and keeping men, as such, alive on the earth. That will be a triumph for God. John intends to show that.

R.B.P. Would you say that the rapture and the resurrection are synchronous ?

J.T. Well, they are for us, but what the Lord is going on to say here goes beyond that. That is, I believe the millennial day is in mind, but we come into something special ; Israel is not, though Israel is in God's purpose, " beloved for the fathers' sakes," Rom. 11 : 28. Things happen to them because of the fathers, but not so to us.

E.P. In relation to your reference to Isaiah 65 : 20 and death as referred to there, do you mean that that is not what will generally obtain in the millennium ? It says there that " the youth shall die a hundred years old." Are you saying that that will not generally obtain ?

J.T. That is a sinner, that if a sinner arises, death will lay hold of him, but generally it is a question of life, and eternal life applies to that period. Eternal life applies to us too, but we are special, it applies in a peculiar way to us, because it leads into the assembly.

Ques. Will the millennial day be just confined to Israel ?

J.T. No, there will be nations as well, and the

nations shall walk in the light of the heavenly city.

S.J.H. When the Lord said to Nicodemus, " If
I have told you earthly things and you believe
not " ; would that include eternal life ?

J.T. That is a question, but I do not believe He
means eternal life, because He is going to speak of
eternal life in the full sense of it. He is going to
speak of it as applicable to the assembly, and that
does not mean it is earthly. He speaks of springing
up ; the fourth chapter shows that the water that
the Lord Jesus gives shall spring up into eternal
life ; " The water that I shall give him shall be in
him a well of water springing up into everlasting
life." So that we have to be cautious and see that
we are saying what is true in the Scriptures ; they
are so broad ; " thy commandment is exceeding
broad," said the psalmist ; Psalm 119 : 96. Sometimes it is wider than at others, so to speak. But
when we come to the assembly we come to the
speciality ; it is the heavenly side of things and
eternal life leads to that. But at the same time
eternal life leads to the millennium, which is the
broadest sense, including the nations, " And the
nations of them which are saved shall walk in the
light of it," Rev. 21 : 24.

F.N.W. The definition of the assembly side of
eternal life has come down to us from Mr. Darby,
I believe. He spoke of the out-of-the-world, heavenly
condition of relationship and being in which eternal
life consists.

J.T. That is right ; that is what I would call
the present application of eternal life, but it has a
wider sense when we come to the millennial day,
because the nations will be included as well, the
nations shall walk in the light of the heavenly city.
The heavenly city is the assembly, but it is in the
heavenly place.

S.McC. In regard to what you said a moment

ago as to the resurrection and what occurs in regard to ourselves as of the assembly, do you look for another operation of resurrection power in regard of Israel following the rapture and before the millennium ?

J.T. I think that is the truth. There will be the application of the idea according to this chapter in the last day. That is not the assembly day, it is the millennial day ; the last day is a very extended idea, it is not a literal day, it is a question of a period of time.

A.N.W. Does not Matthew 25 support your statement that the nations shall come into eternal life ? The nations are brought into it there. The paragraph begins with the Son of man coming in His glory, and " all the nations shall be gathered before him." The section closes with the words, " Then shall he answer them saying, Verily I say to you, Inasmuch as ye have not done it to one of these least, neither have ye done it to me. And these shall go away into eternal punishment, and the righteous into life eternal."

J.T. " Into life eternal," that is very good ; it clarifies the whole position, that eternal life is the thing they go into. The righteous go into it, whereas it says, in chapter 3 as to the persons who die not subject to the Son, that the wrath of God abides on them. The righteous have their own place and they go, not to heaven, but into eternal life.

R.B.P. Then the reference to the last day in John 11, would primarily refer to Israel ?

J.T. That is right, that was what they knew ; that is the thing they were all thinking about, what Israel would come into.

A.R. Would the two resurrections be seen in Revelation 20? " The rest of the dead did not live till the thousand years had been completed. This is the first resurrection. Blessed and holy he who has part in the first resurrection : over these the second death has no power ; but they shall be priests of God and of the Christ, and shall reign with him a thousand years."

J.T. So that the first resurrection is an extended period, just as we were saying ; it is a day, as it were ; many things happen in it. You cannot say that it is a question of a physical day, but a period of time in which things happen. It is classified there as the first resurrection, and blessed are they who have part in that.

G.H. It says in John's epistle, " We know that we have passed from death to life, because we love the brethren." Would that really be eternal life, do you think ?

J.T. That would be what we are enjoying this afternoon, perhaps between the meetings too. It is a question of life functioning as we are together in the Spirit, but that is not the full thought, that is only in principle.

S.McC. In regard to the general teaching in this chapter as to eating the flesh and drinking the blood of the Son of man, is it to prepare us now spiritually and constitutionally in relation to this great thought of change ?

J.T. I was thinking of that. We are quite entitled to take on prophetic subjects as they did at the beginning of the revival in 1825 and 1827 when they had meetings in Dublin to look into the prophetic word. That was quite right, and it opened up the spiritual map to us. But we are not confined to the spiritual map in this day ; we are thinking primarily and almost altogether of the assembly, of our coming into that, and of the service of God, as to our having part in that, carrying on the divine ideas right into the millennium. As engaged with these thoughts we are in our own period. The apostle Paul said, that this salvation is sent to the Gentiles and they will receive it. The Jews rejected it, but the Gentiles would receive it, and we are the Gentiles who have received it ; we are coming into the heavenly part.

S.McC. So that the teaching of this chapter involves the acceptance in our souls of the termination of a certain condition of things, does it not ?

J.T. Well, both things are applicable in this chapter. It is very long and very comprehensive in its contents too, but what we are dealing with now is the prime thought of the assembly, and how this chapter deals with the assembly, and how we may come into the truth of it through the teaching of this chapter.

S.McC. I was thinking of the importance of the teaching to which you are alluding in this chapter, as bearing on the acceptance of it in our souls. It is hard, but as coming into the assembly we have to accept the termination of a certain condition of things, have we not ?

J.T. Yes, quite, but I think the Lord's listeners were turning away because of the things He was saying. They could not follow them, but the question is whether we can follow them and make them good. I may say, I should like to go in for all that, and be truly in the assembly. But am I equal to it ?

A.A.T. You used the expression, *the present period*. How do you cover that period, I mean when does it start ?

J.T. It is the period of the assembly. It started from the time the salvation of God was sent to the Gentiles, from that time in the book of Acts.

A.N.W. That is a period which would not appear on the prophetic map you were speaking of.

J.T. No. I would say in a certain way it may, but strictly speaking it is a period by itself that began not exactly at Pentecost, but when the salvation of God was transferred to the Gentiles. At first it was according to Ephesians, that we *both* might have access, that is, Jew and Gentile, but we would not say that now. The apostle Paul would not say it if he were here. What is in mind now is the Gentiles, there is hardly a Jew in the fellowship. There are one or two here now, and we thank God for them, but there are hardly more than a few. The bulk of the saints are Gentiles, and God is going on with them. It is the time of the Gentiles; "until the time of the Gentiles be fulfilled," Luke 21 : 24.

S.M. Would that be like the day that the Lord has made ?

J.T. "This is the day that Jehovah hath made ; we will rejoice and be glad in it," Psalm 118 : 24.

C.A.M. Referring to the change of condition in this chapter, it has connection with this flesh and blood condition, has it not ? The Lord's flesh and the Lord's blood are separated, which involves a change in the condition of things that we are in at the moment. As to ourselves, does not the eternal life as it is dwelt on here involve our entering in some spiritual sense beyond our present flesh and blood condition ?

J.T. Well, quite so. Peter for instance was in an ecstasy, he got into that condition ; he was outside the reckonings of flesh and blood. That was common in the beginning, but it is not common now as it was then. A wonderful thing that it was so.

C.A.M. Does not the idea of being in an out-of-the-world condition involve something of that ?

J.T. Yes, but it is not an ecstasy, an out-of-the-world condition is a condition that is suitable to us now, in this meeting for instance, or any meeting at all, such as that for the breaking of bread, or the ministry of the truth ; it is an out-of-the-world condition, and the world has no part in it at all. Our attitude is out of the world and that means we are rejected of the world in a moral sense. We are still in flesh and blood, of course, but at the same time we are not moving on that line at all; we have an access to heavenly things, to assembly things, and the more spiritual we are the more we shall enjoy them. It is a question of spirituality, not of literal ecstasy, but of the power of the Spirit in our inmost souls; and the more of us there are together the more it is enjoyed. So that we may say we have enjoyed eternal life this afternoon. We mean it just in a limited way, but it is there; that is to say, the Spirit of God is free amongst us.

H.B. When it is said of Enoch, that he was not, that is a moral idea, is it not?

J.T. Quite so, it means he was taken; God took him, it says. They missed him, I suppose. The neighbours there might miss him and ask, What has become of Enoch? Well, God had taken him. That is the fact the Spirit of God records. But before he was taken or translated " he has the testimony that he had pleased God," Heb. 11 : 5. That is the moral side of it, that is the reason he was translated. What can we say to-day about Enoch or Elijah? We do not know. They are somewhere in the heavenly regions, but we cannot say more than that. Sleeping saints are there too, but not all; some of those that slept arose and came into the holy city, after the Lord's resurrection. How many arose we cannot tell, but they entered into the holy city and appeared to many. What has become of them? We cannot say. God has not been pleased to tell us, but it was true. The point morally is to seek to please God. He is looking for people who seek to please Him.

J.E.P. With regard to the out of the world conditions, the Lord introduces in this chapter the names of all the divine Persons, suggesting to us, would you say, a realm in which divine operations are going forward in a practical way, and we come into that ?

J.T. Yes, I think so ; it is a practical time, and we are called to be practical and simple.

A.N.W. When He that restrains, and that which restrains are gone, things will move rapidly enough ; surely they will move very rapidly when these restraining powers and persons are gone.

J.T. Quite.

S.M. This current exercise about the unions seems to be a special test to us in connection with working for food. The Lord says here, " Work not for the food which perishes." That is the test to us now ; is it not ?

J.T. That is the whole subject, with these unions, it is a question of the food. They are materialistic, but we are to learn to get out of that, we do not belong to that system of things at all.

S.M. We want to please God.

J.T. There is an out-of-the-world, heavenly condition of relationship and being in which eternal life consists. Well, we have part in that, and certainly it is not a question of food and raiment. It is a question of spiritual power and enjoyment implying the fellowship that we come into ; the fellowship of the Spirit it is called.

V.C.L. Verse 35 reads, " And Jesus said to them, I am the bread of life : he that comes to me shall never hunger, and he that believes on me shall never thirst at any time." Would you say a word as to the difference between the not hungering and the not thirsting ?

J.T. It is just a question of the word, either thirst or hunger would have the same force ; it is a question of what is eternal, of what never happens, that we never thirst and we never hunger. Surely that is enough for us, we get that relief in coming to Christ, because it is coming to Him now, it is not simply that He comes to us and takes us to heaven, which He will do, but our coming to Him, involving fellowship.

V.C.L. And does believing on Him involve the Holy Spirit for us ?

J.T. Well, it does; the Spirit would come in to support that faith. But then the idea is faith, whether we do believe, whether we are living in a faith condition. The millennium will not be a faith condition, it will be a condition of sight, but we are living in a faith condition now, so that the end of John's gospel says, " blessed they who have not seen and have believed."

E.A.L. When they said to the Lord, " What should we do that we may work the works of God ? " He answers, " This is the work of God, that ye believe on him whom he has sent."

J.T. That is the work of God, just so, to believe. We are living in a faith condition, whereas the millennium will be a sight condition.

A.R. So we should all be satisfied Christians, should we not ?

J.T. Quite so, never thirsting. We are all made to drink into one Spirit.

J.H.P. Would you say a word about the drawing of the Father ?

J.T. That is the time we are in, the time of this drawing. We are in what is called the expanse. God called the expanse Heaven, and that is the area or region in which He is operating and we are in that now. It is a period of faith for us. The Old Testament was not that and the millennium will not be that, but for us it is a question of whether we are living by faith or by sight.

Ques. Is the period of faith, then, in some degree greater than the period of sight ?

J.T. Oh, it is, clearly, that is what the Lord is

saying here, that blessedness lies in those who believe without seeing.

L.L.P. Would the dignitaries of chapter 11 of Hebrews have reached beyond their dispensation; that is, do they belong to ours ?

J.T. They anticipated our dispensation. The word *faith* governs all that section. They cannot be perfect without us ; that is what the apostle says, " that they without us should not be made perfect." That shows the greatness of ourselves ; that is of the assembly.

G.H. Do you mean that the expanse in Genesis 1 is like the period of faith ?

J.T. No, that is not the idea, but it corresponds, it is the same idea as the expanse. He called the expanse Heavens. That was the area of God's operations then, but it is a question of what He is doing now ; He is gathering out the assembly ; that is what He is doing. Earlier than this, He was gathering out Israel, and many other things He was doing in the Old Testament times.

E.A.L. Would you say then that prophecy in ministry is an expansive idea, always expanding, so that we shall always be learning ?

J.T. That is the idea. The word here is : " And they shall be all taught of God." That peculiarly applies to ourselves now.

S.McC. In connection with this food, He speaks of the bread of life, the bread from heaven, and of eating the flesh and drinking the blood of the Son of man. What distinction do you make in regard to these suggestions of food ?

J.T. It is a question of appropriation, eating is just a question of appropriation, but it is a most vivid feature or picture of it. Are we appropriating what is within our reach ? This chapter shows what is within our reach, and the greatest matter is the flesh of Christ and the blood of Christ. That is not the Lord's supper; the Lord distinguishes that from His Supper, although it bears on it.

E.P. Does eating the flesh of the Son of man and drinking His blood go beyond the type of the manna?

J.T. Certainly. It says, " Your fathers ate the manna in the wilderness and died ; but then the Son of man has come in and He must be greater than everything else and every other person.

S.McC. Would the bread from heaven have the positive side more in mind, but the flesh of the Son of man more the negative side ; that is, the ending of a certain condition of things ?

J.T. I think the word *heaven* must have some weight there, bread from heaven shows the character of it, but then the flesh of Christ and the blood of Christ is a matter of literality, it involves that the Lord actually died. We are to appropriate it in the negative sense to separate us from the world.

A.N.W. In that way would it not negative such an idea as that in verse 42 for instance, which might be in any mind ? " And they said, Is not this Jesus the son of Joseph, whose father and mother we have known ? "

J.T. That was all they had in their minds, that He was no different from anybody else, whereas we are dealing now with the spiritual side of things, and when the Lord speaks about His flesh being bread we have to see that it is a question of spiritual food which we appropriate for sustenance. Eating is simply a figure of appropriation, appropriating something that the Lord Jesus has provided for us in coming down from heaven and dying.

A.A.T. Is there something in its being said, that it is the flesh of the Son of man ?

J.T. We have often spoken about the use of that title in Ezekiel, that it is a question of the Lord's relations with man, and not simply with the Jews. If the Jews are to come into it at all they have to take the ground of being men ; God will allow that they shall come into the period that refers to the Son of man ; the Son of man's period.

A.R. In regard to this matter of appropriation of the flesh and the blood, it is after He is dead, is it not ? So that it is important to realise that we appropriate a dead Christ.

J.T. It has often been said that what is before us in the Lord's supper is a dead Christ. We come later in the service to a living Christ, gone up into heaven : " And has raised us up together, and has made us sit down together in the heavenlies in Christ Jesus."

McC. What is the force of verse 54, " He that eats my flesh and drinks my blood has life eternal, and I will raise him up at the last day " ?

J.T. That means that you appropriate for two things ; you appropriate for support in the sense of strength, and then you appropriate what satisfies you morally ; that is, you are not dissatisfied, complaining ; you are free ; you are fully satisfied.

Mc.C. How does eternal life come into that ?

J.T. That is the point, that there is satisfaction in the sense of strength, the bread to strengthen man's heart ; but then wine is to make his heart glad.

B.W. Would you say a person that is satisfied with divine things is in the good of eternal life ?

J.T. Just so, he has means, he is not a theorist. You do not look at your bank book to satisfy yourself. You have food to satisfy you without anything else, the food the Lord supplies for you, and it is no less than Himself, His own body ; that is to say He has died for us, as Paul says, He " loved me and gave himself for me."

W.W. We might be like the disciples on the line of unbelief, and saying, " This is a hard saying." His own disciples said that.

J.T. Just so, but Peter gives the answer, as if he were the great answerer of questions as to the Lord. He said, " Lord, to whom shall we go ? thou hast words of life eternal." That is what I was trying to say in the beginning, that we are dealing with words, not simply with paragraphs but the actual words, and they are words of life, words of eternal life.

S.McC. In verse 57, the Lord Jesus says, " As the living Father has sent me and I live on account of the Father, he also who eats me shall live also on account of me." Does the eating Him there refer to the appropriation of Christ as He now is ?

J.T. I think the truth is advancing in this chapter; it is ' higher and higher yet,' and when we come to the Father and the Son, and how the Father suggests the Son as food, I mean the life of Christ and the death of Christ, if the Father speaks about that we are on a higher level. They are acting together, and we are coming into what the action is ; " he that eats my flesh and drinks my blood has life eternal." And then verse 57, " As the living Father has sent me and I live on account of the Father, he also who eats me shall live also on account of me." That is a higher thought, that is my position now, not simply that I am in fellowship, but I eat Christ ; the Father gives me that food. The Lord says, " I live on account of the Father," and we live on account of Christ. That is the word, " on account of." The Lord says, " as the living Father has sent me, and I live on account of the Father, he also who eats me shall live also on account of me." Notice " the living Father," it is a remarkable thought ; not simply the Father, but " the living Father " and then " on account of." So that I am living on account of Christ or by virtue of the fact that He has supplied this food for me. It is the very highest level, you might say, as to eating.

S.McC. What you have said is very helpful. It involves Christ in glory, does it not ?

J.T. Just so ; coming down to where we are and providing food for us in that living way. " The living Father." I do not know that I ever noticed it more than I do now, that it is the title, " *living Father*."

R.P. Say a little more as to it.

J.T. Well, I do not know what to say, there it is, just one of the things that enters into this long chapter that is so precious, because it is a leading up, it is a steady leading up to the higher level in John 6. There are 71 verses about this great subject so that we should be entirely here on account of the Father, here in life as living people by the Father's power.

V.C.L. In verse 32, it says, " my Father gives you the true bread out of heaven," but in verse 58, " This is the bread which has come down out of heaven," as though it would be something further.

J.T. It is further. It is a further thought in the chapter ; this matter of the living Father and living on account of the Father, all that wording is what we might call ' higher and higher yet.' The chapter ascends as we go to the very highest level short of the assembly and the heavenly side of the truth. So that there is no difference at all between the heavens and the earth in that sense, we go out of the earthly side into the heavenly ; our place is heaven. He has raised us up together and made us to sit down together in the heavenlies in Christ.

W.S. Does Mr. Darby's note help in that connection ? It reads, as to the expression " on account of," the sense is, ' by reason of what the Father is and His living, that I live by reason of His being and living.'

J.T. Very good, showing the high level we are on now.

S.McC. What you said a little while ago, helps as to the heavenly bearing of eternal life in John's gospel, while it is for the earth. Is there not a distinctive heavenly touch in John's gospel in relation to eternal life ?

J.T. There is a heavenly touch ; that is why it is brought in, I think, in chapter 3, as to " the Son of man who is in heaven " ; the Son of man, mark, not the Son of God, but the Son of man. His real manhood is implied, and that He is in heaven. It is a mysterious thing.

S.McC. So that eternal life as we enjoy it now in the assembly is really on a much higher plane and level than it will be in the millennium.

J.T. That is just the truth. It is on a higher level than it will be in the millennium. The millennium is part of the division of time, you might say, the seventh day ; it is the last day here in this chapter. As linked with the first of Genesis it belongs to the great period of divine operations in the expanse.

J.H.P. Is the high level that you speak of seen in the last sentence of verse 58, " he that eats this bread shall live for ever " ?

J.T. Quite so. " He that eats this bread."

A.A.T. In an afternoon like this, do we touch heaven ?

J.T. We do touch heaven, because the Spirit of God is here, and if He is amongst us, He brings everything with Him. You cannot add to or subtract from a divine Person ; He brings everything with Him. If the Lord was here, He would bring everything with Him, and so with the Father. Divine Persons take you to finality and totality. When we come to the eternal state of things, they will all be there, and there abidingly, eternally, and we shall be there too.

J.K.P. There is a distinct contrast in verse 58 between the old dispensation in which it says your fathers ate and died, and this special dispensation to which I understand you are referring now, in which death is not introduced at all morally. It is a question of living for ever.

J.T. Quite so, we touch that too in some little degree ; it is always a small degree, we may say, but it is wonderful that it can be touched. Take Peter, he was in an ecstasy, he was waiting for a meal, and he said in effect, I will go upstairs and pray, and as he did so he became in an ecstasy. Well, it is wonderful that that could have happened. That is the beginning of the dispensation we are in now. It has nearly ended, but that is what was at the beginning ; so that we have to watch and see the possibilities.

E.P. You mean that we touch eternal conditions and that is what really gives character to eternal life here.

J.T. That is so, and the assembly is no less than that, it is no less than the place where we enjoy eternal conditions. It is never an earthly thing, it is a heavenly thing, the house of God is heavenly.

S.McC. So that in the assembly properly speaking death does not exist ; it is a deathless state of things properly speaking ?

J.T. Just so, deathless. That is a fine expression ; we used it years ago. We have come into a deathless condition spiritually.

E.P. "And everyone who lives and believes on me shall never die," John 11 : 26. Is that our outlook ?

J.T. That is the idea exactly, "never die."

A.D. So the Lord says later on in chapter 17, "I am no longer in the world, and these are in the world, and I come to thee. Holy Father, keep them in thy name which thou hast given me, that they may be one as we."

J.T. John 17 is a wonderful chapter, one of the most

wonderful, it is the Lord's prayer, not the one that you get in Matthew. John 17 is the Lord's own prayer.

S.J.H. Do I understand you to say the title "living Father" is peculiar to our dispensation?

J.T. I do not know where else it is, I am not sure that it is elsewhere; it just comes in here with a peculiar touch to emphasise the Father, He is the living Father, He is the living God too, but this gives an added touch to what is said.

JOHN 7 : 37–39 ; REVELATION 1 : 9–20 ; 3 : 7–13

J.T. Our subject now is not to be based simply on the scriptures read ; our subject is the Spirit of God Himself in view of what has come to the attention of the brethren for some months past, that there might be a clarification of it in our minds, and a readiness to give the Holy Spirit His place as a divine Person, as equal with the Father and with the Son. And so many scriptures will doubtless come before us in this inquiry. However, certain things that are outstanding ought to be remarked, and one is that the Old Testament has the same value as the New Testament. The value of the Old Testament is that it is Scripture, and the Scripture says itself, " Every scripture is divinely inspired, and profitable for teaching, for conviction, for correction, for instruction in righteousness ; that the man of God may be complete, fully fitted to every good work," 2 Tim. 3 : 16, 17. The Old Testament therefore should come into view a little, particularly the first chapter of the Bible, that is the first of Genesis, and then some passages in the book of Ezekiel where a great deal is said about the Spirit of God, and of speaking to Him, and of His speaking to others. In the New Testament, in the book of Acts, in the section referring to the introduction of the Gentiles, we have the Spirit speaking to Peter, although it does not say definitely at first that the Spirit spoke to him, but clearly the voice is the Spirit's voice, the context shows it, that the Spirit is speaking to Peter, and Peter speaks to the Spirit. That is a point that we ought to get clear about. Moreover it is said in the book of Revelation, in chapter 14, that a voice is heard from heaven. " Blessed the

dead who die in the Lord from henceforth." That
voice clearly bears on the Spirit, because the Spirit
answers immediately as if the voice were to Him,
" Yea, saith the Spirit, that they may rest from
their labours." These are only illustrations of what
may be said as to the blessed Spirit of God as an
Object of conversation on our part ; that is, to be
conversed with. In type Genesis 24 is very clear
that the chief servant of Abraham is a type of the
Holy Spirit, and that He conversed with Rebecca,
that is to say, the Holy Spirit in type conversed
with Rebecca who is a type of the assembly. Well,
many other passages might be introduced, but
I believe what is said is enough now to have in our
minds, so that the Spirit may have His full place
with us. He has it among the saints in general,
so far as I can hear, particularly in this country,
and in Australasia, and in the British Isles, and so
far as I know on the continent of Europe too, and
in the West Indies. The general thought of con-
versing with the Spirit is laid hold of and practised
and enjoyed. The brethren are speaking of having
great enjoyment in the fellowship that they have
with the blessed Spirit of God, and why should they
not have, because the Spirit of God can help us, and
does help us, He adds His help to our weaknesses.

J.S.Sr. Would Matthew 5 : 17 help us in connection with establishing the Old and New Testaments
on the same basis. " Think not that I am come to
make void the law or the prophets ; I am not come
to make void, but to fulfil."

J.T. Very good.

W.A.T. It has been sometimes said that Paul
did not say much about the Spirit on the line on
which we are now speaking, but one has noticed
how he does give place to the Spirit in this way.
Just to mention one instance in Isaiah 6, it says,
" I heard the voice of the Lord saying, " Go and

thou shalt say unto this people." When Paul quotes that in Acts 28, he says, "Well spoke the Holy Spirit," suggesting thus that the Holy Spirit is speaking to-day and Paul is making much of that ?

J.T. Quite so ; you get many instances of that kind, where the Holy Spirit is used to convey the scriptures of the Old Testament, as for instance in Hebrews 10.

S.McC. Is it not interesting that in the section read in John 7 the matter as to the Spirit comes up in relation to Jesus teaching in the temple ? Much has been made in the recovery of the truth in our day as to the temple and teaching in that light. In verse 14, "Jesus went up into the temple and taught." He is teaching in the temple. We get letters from all parts inquiring as to this matter of the Spirit, but do you not think it is important that the brethren should see the gain of inquiring as to it in relation to the temple ?

J.T. I would refer to Luke 2 in regard to that, as to Simeon ; he came by the Spirit into the temple, he is a man in Jerusalem, a characteristic man in Jerusalem and he came by the Spirit into the temple ; and when he came Mary and Joseph brought in the Lord Jesus, and he took the Lord Jesus into his arms and blessed them. He blessed *them*.

A.R. Is not this matter of speaking to the Spirit as seen in Acts 10, worth reading ? It says in verse 13, "And there was a voice to him, Rise, Peter, slay and eat. And Peter said, In no wise, Lord ; for I have never eaten anything common or unclean. And there was a voice again the second time, to him, What God has cleansed, do not thou make common." Then it goes on to say in verse 19, "But as Peter continued pondering over the vision, the Spirit said to him, Behold, three men seek thee ; but rise up, go down, and go with them, nothing doubting, because I have sent them." That clearly shows there was a conversation going on between the Spirit and Peter.

J.T. I would say that clearly.

S.McC. It is rather interesting that in John 7 we have not a direct text quoted, but the Lord says, " He that believes on me, as the scripture has said, out of his belly shall flow rivers of living water."

J.T. The Lord leaves it open, and He is saying in effect to us this afternoon, Why do you not study your Bibles, and see if you can find that scripture ? I think we can ; I believe we have not far to go. In Genesis 24, Isaac was coming and going from the well. There are many wells in Genesis, and there we begin with the thought of rivers ; and there are other such scriptures to indicate that the idea of rivers is important in the Old Testament, and they are alluded to in this chapter ; the Lord Himself stressing for our benefit, that the Scriptures have said so and so, and that if we look into them we shall find that it is so. The Lord did not mean anything else but that the Scriptures were findable.

Rem. The footnote on the word *believe* indicates that it is ' characteristically believing.' " He that believes," is characteristic. Is that state necessary in order to reach the great truth as to addressing the Spirit ?

J.T. Just so. It is, as it were, round about the Spirit, the Spirit is the centre of things, the centre of the inquiry. The subject is the Spirit really, " But this he said concerning the Spirit."

J.H.P. Does not the expression " Jesus stood and cried," suggest how urgent a matter this is, and how we should move quickly as to it ?

J.T. Yes. These phrases are so unusual that the Lord should be seen standing and crying. You find it in some other instances, but not many. I am glad you mentioned it ; it is very urgent.

S.J.H. Would you say, that the last, the great day, was very empty actually, but the Lord is bringing in at the last, in the great day, these very choice things ?

J.T. He has something great to bring in, the word *great* is not to be overlooked, the Lord has something great to say Himself as to what He had in His mind. He had said already that " the scripture has said," but He Himself had something great to say, He had what we are engaged with this afternoon, and what has been engaging us for months past, and do not we all regard it as great ?

S.J.H. I was thinking of that, and the fact of urgency being mentioned ; it is the last day, and as we think to be near the end, the choicest things are coming out.

S.McC. It is very interesting, that in the climax of the revival in Nehemiah the culminating point of the first choir in chapter 12 are the fountain gate and the water gate, eastward. Does that not fit in with the present moment in the truth ?

J.T. I think the Lord would say that is right, and I would follow what I believe the Lord would say, that there is much in that suggestion as to these gates. Linking on with Genesis 24, the idea of water there is very prominent, and Isaac was occupied with it really, he was coming and going to the well Beer-lahai-roi, occupied with it at that particular time.

A.R. The revival took place in Ezra and Nehemiah in the days of the feast of tabernacles, and the same idea is in this chapter. It is the feast of tabernacles, like the end of the dispensation, is it not ?

J.T. Yes, quite so, the feast of tabernacles is the last of the feasts.

A.R. I was wondering if it fits in with what you were saying yesterday about the seventh day ?

J.T. It does.

L.L.P. Would you attach any importance to the fact that some of the most outstanding women in the Scriptures got their start at wells ?

J.T. I believe you are right. We have been looking at that in New York; the types of the assembly in the whole Bible, beginning at the first of Genesis with Adam and Eve, and it is remarkable how many women are seen at wells, identified with water.

L.L.P. Yes, Leah and Rebecca ; and Moses, too, met his wife Zipporah at a well. He served her, and his father-in-law was a man that was able to link on and give his daughter a right start and a right link. And then with Rebecca, the servant tested her at the well, as to whether she fitted in with what he required.

J.T. In the fourth of John, there is another.

A.N.W. Would Achsah be on that line ?

J.H.P. Rachel was connected with a well, and she was a shepherdess.

J.T. A shepherdess, quite so. Jacob rolled away the stone from the well as soon as she came to light.

A.B. In the end of John 4 which we did not read, the Lord would seem to make it urgent to the disciples that the reaping time is here. I wondered whether in the last twenty years we have perhaps had the reaping in relation to the Father, and then later to the Son, and whether this might not be the last field to be reaped.

J.T. The field of the Spirit, very good. I hope we all understand that. Now you have to say a little more because it is all so vast.

A.B. I just wondered whether this field in relation to the Spirit might not be the last field to be reaped, and therefore it is an urgent matter.

J.T. I think it is very urgent ; and another thing I am reminded of, the order in which these great subjects have come out. We had eternal life before most of us were in the field at all, and we have been engaged with it for a long time. Then after that we had the sonship of Christ ; we used to speak of the eternal Son, but that has been set aside, for the sonship of Christ refers to Him in manhood, not in the eternal state at all, but in manhood. So that we may say the first field is eternal life, and the second field is the sonship of Christ, and now this third field is the Spirit of God, and we want to get the full bearing of that this afternoon.

A.N.W. If we could only be gleaners ! The word was to the gleaners to go to no other field, but glean where the reapers are.

J.T. The field of Boaz.

W.P. In relation to the urgency of the matter, is it not interesting that three of the types in the Old Testament were seen in peculiar activity ? Rebecca was one, and Achsah was another, and Abigail was another. Do they help us to see the urgency with which matters are to be taken on ?

J.T. They do.

A.R. Do you think the urgency of this matter of the Spirit is in view of the rapture ?

J.T. I think so.

W.A.T. Regarding the order of Genesis 26 following chapter 24, which brings to light the assembly, in chapter 26 the wells are dug, suggesting that that is the way the truth has come out to-day, like the new well that was dug, would you say ?

J.T. Quite so ; and Isaac named that well the Broadways ; so that things are enlarged in chapter 26. The wells that Abraham had dug were closed up, the Philistines had done that, but Isaac was opening them up again, and in his services God helps him to get to the Broadways. There is plenty of liberty now in this new well that is opened up. And then another thing in that chapter is that the Philistines came to see Isaac and he sent them away ; he had moral power to send them away, and they went away in peace from him. The idea in our meetings is to promote peace, not strife, but peace.

E.T. Is this expression, " out of his belly," linked up with the idea of assimilation ? It is not out of his head, it is out of his belly.

J.T. Well, quite so. It comes from the inwards where nourishment is yielded, and where the strength comes from ; that is what the idea is I think, that there is something coming out in power. It is not that we are weaklings. It is the believer that is alluded to here ; " he that believes " ; he is in power, he is not a weakling, he did not come just yesterday. In fact he is like Ittai the Gittite, he was going with David anyway. David says, ' You came to us but yesterday ' ; but he says, ' I want to be with you.' He had power.

Ques. Does the fact that the Lord speak of the Spirit on the last day suggest that there is something lacking, and the Spirit is intended to supply that ?

J.T. The whole position amongst the Jews at that time was empty. What was there ? And so in the second of Acts it was as the feast of Pentecost was running its course, that the Spirit came in at that point, the mighty voice from heaven was heard, and it was like unto the hard breathing of God, so as to announce the wonderful fact that the dispensation was inaugurated.

S.McC. Do you think that we need to be like Ezekiel, amenable to leadership in relation to the truth ? In the latter part of Ezekiel, he is led in, he is led around, he is led without, but the last feature of movement is in chapter 47, " And he brought me back to the door of the house ; and behold, waters issued." The last feature of turning and movement is connected with what suggests the Spirit.

J.T. Those rivers, undoubtedly suggest the very

78

thing that is in mind here in John 7 ; the very thing
that we did not know, but that the Lord meant to
convey. I believe, it is suggested in Ezekiel, in the
waters to swim in, a river that could not be passed
over ; what can we get more than that to illustrate
the idea of rivers flowing out ?

B.W. Would 1 Corinthians 2 have a bearing on
that, communicating spiritual things by spiritual
means ? The communicating there is expounding,
and I was thinking of what comes to light in a time
like this and the authority of it.

J.T. " Spiritual means " ; that means that we
are able to converse profitably, and I might say
intelligently. I do not believe that readings of this
type especially marked the beginning of Christianity,
but they are much in evidence now ; the revival has
brought them out. These are conversational meetings,
and this conversational ministry is mentioned in
Acts 20. We are in the time of conversational
ministry, and it means that the persons who take
part in these readings have intelligence and are able
to communicate with one another, as it says in the
next to the last chapter of the Old Testament, " Then
they that feared Jehovah spoke often one to another ;
and Jehovah observed it, and heard."

B.W. It goes on to say in that scripture in
Corinthians, " But the natural man does not receive
the things of the Spirit of God, for they are folly to
him ; and he cannot know them because they are
spiritually discerned."

J.T. That is a good passage to govern our readings
as we call them.

L.W. Is there a suggestion as to the activity of
the Spirit in verse 20 of Exodus 23 ? " Behold, I
send an angel before thee, to keep thee in the way,
and to bring thee to the place that I have prepared.
Be careful in his presence, and hearken unto his
voice : do not provoke him, for he will not forgive

your transgressions ; for my name is in him. But if thou shalt diligently hearken unto his voice, and do all that I shall say, then I will be an enemy to thine enemies, and an adversary to thine adversaries."

J.T. That is an allusion undoubtedly to the Spirit ; I think, however, that it is an Angel ; the Spirit is kept more or less out of view, the Angel is in mind. He has to be regarded, they have to be careful in his presence, because he is not empty handed. I think it has direct application to the exact time that it was written, but its application typically is to what we are going through now, only that the Spirit is keeping Himself out of view, as it were, because it is an Angel that is in mind.

S.J.H. In reference to the rivers, would it be right to take the view that the recovery will be so complete that we shall get back to the thought of God in the four rivers that came out of Eden ?

J.T. That helps. Why do we not think of these things ? The Lord would say to us, You are inquiring about John 7, but when I spoke about rivers of living water, why did you not think about those rivers in Genesis and Ezekiel ? So that the Scriptures are full of what the Lord had in mind.

F.N.W. You were referring to Genesis 26, and there is a well dug at the end of that chapter following the ones that are named. Is it indicated that that might be Isaac's well, not one of Abraham's that is redug ? Do you feel that the help we are receiving as to the Holy Spirit now is distinctive to this time, or is it a redigging of what was known in the apostles' days ?

J.T. I do not know whether I could show from the Scriptures that it was known then, although I think what Peter says would indicate that he knew, for the Spirit was speaking and he spoke to Him. I think that is the truth.

E.A.L. Stephen was called a man full of faith and the Holy Spirit, and he says, " O stiff-necked and uncircumcised in heart and ears, ye do always resist the Holy Spirit ; as your fathers, ye also." Some to-day seem to recognise the types that we speak of, such as the type in Genesis 24, but then they say that the types are being taken out of their scope. Has not ministry helped us to see that we cannot limit the scope of what divine Persons may do ? Is that not really an uncircumcised heart operating ? I mean they are not taking on the truth because they are resisting it.

J.T. Yes, they are letting the Old Testament go, so to speak, and reducing it to a lower level than the New Testament. I know, because I have had to do with them. One of the first things I had to do with in the matter was in John 10, where they said to the Lord that He blasphemed because He said He was the Son of God. But the Lord says, that " If he called them gods to whom the word of God came, . . . do ye say of him whom the Father has sanctified and sent into the world, Thou blasphemest, because I said, I am Son of God ? " The Lord makes the point that it is a question of words, and the Lord is convicting them of violating Scripture, so He says, " the scripture cannot be broken," and that is the great word, " the scripture cannot be broken." The Old Testament is the Scripture, and it cannot be broken.

McC. And so the Lord is referring here to the Old Testament Scriptures.

J.T. There were none others when the Lord was here, and then after the Lord arose there were none others, and after He went to heaven there were very few, and then the Scriptures began to be written.

A.C.W. In 1 Timothy 4 we read, " But the Spirit speaks expressly, that in latter times some shall apostatise from the faith, giving their mind to deceiving spirits and teachings of demons." The Spirit is speaking there expressly.

J.T. The Spirit speaks expressly, quite so.

E.P. In relation to our brother's question as to this truth being known in apostolic days are we not being recovered to the truth as it was in the beginning? It seems in the book of Acts that persons were very familiar with the Spirit and His movements in the testimony?

J.T. Well, no doubt, we are being recovered, but I would not make it entirely what is recovered, because there are fresh things coming out; the Lord has been reserving things to bring them out in view of the end. Of course the word in Isaiah applies in a general way, " a remnant shall return "; that is what Shear-jashub means. That is the burden of the book of Isaiah, but then we do not need to limit ourselves to the idea of remnant, because God is God, and He is insisting on the fact that He is God; and the Holy Spirit is God, and the three Persons are, each one of Them God, for there is only one God; and there are fresh things coming out, things that perhaps the early Christians did not touch; and why should we not allow that liberty to the Lord in our day?

W.W. It is a great thing to see that God is not limited to what was formerly known; it is a question of accumulation, and God never returns to just the previous status, does He? He always brings out something more.

J.T. Quite so, why should He not?

A.P. In the formula for baptism, baptising them " to the name of the Father, and of the Son, and of the Holy Spirit, does not that involve the knowledge of each divine Person; and severally, and in the order in which they come? Our knowledge of Them seems to follow that order.

J.T. Quite so, you cannot reverse that order;

you could not begin with the Spirit, and go back to the Father. You begin with the Father. It is to the name of the Father and of the Son and of the Holy Spirit ; there is only one name, it is one God in the three Persons.

W.A.T. So that now we are getting an increased knowledge of the Holy Spirit.

J.T. I think so ; I think when we baptise now, we have a little more light and power in the baptism. You take up the child with more tenderness, I believe, and more feeling, and baptise it *to* the name of the Father ; it is not *in* the name there, it is *to*, as if to put the child into the presence of God. It is " to the name of the Father, and of the Son, and of the Holy Spirit."

W.A.T. As to this question of speaking to the Spirit, is it not a matter of desire, the desire of the soul to give to a divine Person what is due to Him in worship ? In these verses you have read it says, " If any one thirst, let him come to me," and then it adds, " this he said concerning the Spirit." Is it not a question of really thirsting in one's soul to render to a divine Person what is due to Him ?

J.T. Quite so : " Hast thou heard of never thirsting," as the hymn puts it. These wonderful things belong to poetry and God may help us to write poetry so that we may sing better.

A.R. In regard to the service of God there is quite an exercise at the present time as to how we should speak to the Spirit and when.

J.T. I think if you take the order of the service, the Lord's supper is, of course, the very foundation of our position ; it is the very centre of it. The term refers to the Lord ; it does not refer to the Spirit, it does not refer to the Father, it refers to the Lord, it is the Lord's supper. We cannot speak of the Father's supper, or the Spirit's supper ; it is the Lord's supper, and we go through with that rightly first, then we have liberty otherwise. If we want to speak to the Father, we do, and we may speak about the Son; we may speak about Him, but I would say, we should be sparse in doing it. I think what we have been doing for many years is pretty nearly right, that the Father is the ultimate of everything, the Father in the economy is the ultimate of everything, and therefore we proceed with the Father and end with the Father. And this, of course, leads to God, " that God may be all in all."

R.P. Just when would we speak to the Spirit?

J.T. Any time. I do not see that we should limit it in that sense, He is the Spirit of God, a divine Person. If you are led to do it, bearing in mind what we have said about the Lord's supper, there is no reason why you might not allude, for instance, to the Spirit of adoption, because that is a term that is applicable.

Ques. I suppose we should rightly differentiate between those who are inquiring in a godly and reverential way as to the matter of addressing the Holy Spirit, and those who are criticising. I am one who, heretofore, had not seen the matter clearly. I should say, that up till to-day, I had been looking for the basis of address to the Holy Spirit; but I have been doing it I trust soberly.

A.N.W. Was it not your point, that in Genesis 26, some of the wells were an occasion of contention, but this matter is not a matter of contention?

J.T. We have come to broadways. We have no contention here to-day.

Rem. Ephesians 1 : 14, would bear out what has been said as to worshipping the Spirit; it says, " to the praise of his glory," referring as I have heard you say, to the Holy Spirit of promise in verse 13.

J.T. Quite so. Relative to the remarks of our brother here, I think that what has been said as to

Broadways implies richness, a certain richness and liberty of soul, and you are much more likely to bear with people when you are in that state than when you are not so free and easy. One has used the expression, being on easy terms with God, and I think it is a very good expression; and then we may be on easy terms with the Spirit, and on easy terms with the Lord Jesus, and on easy terms with the brethren too. You will not go very far in speaking rashly or too tersely to them if you are on these lines. You want to go as far as you can with them.

A.N.W. May I just read that last word about the Broadways? "And he called the name of it Rehoboth" (which means Broadways), "and said, For now Jehovah has made room for us, and we shall be fruitful in the land."

J.T. Very good.

Rem. I was much impressed that at the meetings at Plainfield you said that the brethren need to have patience with one another in regard to this matter of the Holy Spirit.

J.T. Quite so.

J.H.P. As our time is nearly gone, would you tell us what you had in mind as to the passages in Revelation?

J.T. It was just to bring out the place the Spirit has in the Lord's own remarks. As we know the book of Revelation was given to Christ by God. It is a remarkable thing that God gave it to Him to show to His servants things which must shortly come to pass, and amongst these things that John was to write were "what thou hast seen," but particularly as to now, "the things that are." We have read from the things that are, meaning the addresses to certain assemblies, amongst which is the assembly of Philadelphia; and the most precious address of all is the one to that assembly, because in that connection the great revival has worked out. The Lord says to her, " I also will keep thee out of the hour of trial, which is about to come upon the whole habitable world, to try them that dwell upon the earth." The Lord says that to Philadelphia, and we are learning something of the meaning of Philadelphia. I mean to say, what the name means ; brotherly love, and it is very precious that it does, and we should be in brotherly love. The Broadways makes way for it. But as we were saying, " the things that are " refer to the addresses to the assemblies, and that to Philadelphia is one of the most precious addresses that we have. The Lord says, to that assembly, which would mean the assembly in our day, " I also will keep thee out of the hour of trial, which is about to come upon the whole habitable world, to try them that dwell upon the earth." So that is a promise, and a most comforting promise, that whatever happens in regard to trade unionism or any other ism that is a trial to us, the Lord says ' I will keep thee from it.' I would think that He means that we are to be kept out of it, not simply from it, but out of it, by being transferred to heaven, and it is a great comfort to have that in our minds. That is why I suggested that we should read these few verses.

W.McK. Does that promise apply in prinicple at the present time ? The Lord does not say that He will *take* them out of it, but if the saints are faithful in the things they have to go through such as you have mentioned, the Lord says He will *keep* them out of it.

J.T. Yes, I think that is right too. I am glad you mentioned that ; but I do believe, that the Lord really means that He will take us out of it by taking us up to heaven.

W.McK. Yes, I see that, but I was only thinking of a present application of the word.

J.T. You have experienced that, and you have been kept out of it. I think it ought to be understood that although the trade unions are now pretty stiff, and employment is not so full as it was, at the same time at bottom there is a secret understanding, especially in some parts, that if a man has a conscience, they will recognise it. I do not know whether you would confirm that ?

W.McK. I have had to do with that, and one of the things that the business agent said was, This man has a conscience and has a right to be respected.

J.T. Very good. That is what is meant, and I believe if others of our brethren in the New York area will take that ground, God will be with them. Moreover certain letters that I have seen show that the Senators are sympathetic with the idea of the refusal of the closed shop.

A.N.W. We saw a letter from a senator in which he used the words, ' We are very much concerned about the matter,' showing his sympathy for the brethren.

J.T. That would indicate that God is perhaps in the thing. We are not politicians of course at all, we are Christians, and we are dealing with our own matters now ; but at the same time the powers that be are our matters too, that we respect the powers that be. They are the law makers, there must be laws, and we are glad there are, and they make them, and we have access to these men. If we were simply to say, I know of a man who cannot get work because the trades union will not let him, the senators might be helped to suggest something that would lead to the brethren getting work without difficulty.

V.C.L. Do you not think that the understanding of the Spirit's place as the Comforter is peculiarly intended to strengthen us at a time like this, when we may be able to prove Him in that capacity as perhaps we have not known Him before ?

J.T.   That is to say, He is in charge of our affairs down here as the Lord is in charge of our affairs in heaven.   There may be opposition up there too from the devil but the Spirit is in charge of our affairs down here on the earth, and we see that He is working in our favour ;   we count on Him to influence the authorities.   But we should also see that there is such a thing as angelic service, which I believe is very much ignored amongst the brethren.   They are said to be all ministering spirits, sent out to minister on account of those who shall be heirs of salvation ; and that ministering is very largely a question of interference in connection with our external matters, as for instance one angel destroyed 85,000 men in the days of the Old Testament.   So that we may count on God doing things for us not only by the Spirit but by angelic service.

R.P.   Why is the Spirit so prominent in these early chapters of Revelation ?

J.T.   Because it is a question of what the Lord Himself has been given, the revelation which God has given to Christ, " to show to his bondmen what must shortly take place."   He sent and signified it ;   the word *signified* means that it is in signs, there are significations and signs ;   and He sent and signified it by His servant John to His servants. John is viewed as a bondman in this book, he takes a lowly place ;   he says, " I John, your brother and fellow-partaker in the tribulation, and kingdom and patience, in Jesus."   Then he tell us that he was in the Spirit on the Lord's day ;   much is made of the Spirit, and then he tells us that he heard a voice behind him, and it comes to light that the Lord is acting judicially in this first chapter.   In the second chapter the Lord says, " He that has an ear, let him hear what the Spirit says to the assemblies." The Lord says, so to speak, ' I am saying so much, but the Spirit could say much more ;   He would open up and enlarge on what I have said.' That is the ministry of it.

W.McK. Does the fact that John denotes himself as a brother and fellow-partaker before he says, " I became in the Spirit," show what is possible for us ?

J.T. Quite so.

R.P. The Spirit now to-day is adding to what has been said, is that your thought ?

J.T. That is the idea. You might say, The Lord has said all that is to be said, He has written seven epistles to the assemblies. Why do they not contain all that is to be said ? But then the Lord has not said everything ; He is leaving something to the Spirit ; so that we have ministry, we have meetings like this, and the Spirit speaks. It says, " let him hear what the Spirit says," not what the Lord says, but what the Spirit says to the assemblies.

Rem. That is still continuing is it not ?

J.T. Yes it is. We have our Bibles open, and one and another is saying something, and the Spirit is helping us to do it.

A.R. These letters that are being written to Washington are not being written to politicians ; it is a question of recognising and writing to the government, is it not ?

J.T. Quite so, and if we do not recognise that, we are not recognising the truth, because it is part of the truth, and it dates back to Nebuchadnezzar, when God handed over the government of the world to him ; and this goes on still. Why should we not observe that, and recognise these facts ? We are not politicians, we are simply acting wisely, we see our brethren suffering and we want to help them.

H.B. In the second chapter of the Song of Solomon where the beloved says to the spouse, " And the voice of the turtle dove is heard in *our* land." Is that an allusion to the Spirit, do you think ? Would the turtle dove typically suggest the Spirit, the form in which He would come down ?

J.T. Noah too had to do with that ; the dove is mentioned in connection with him. It has to do with the blessed Lord Jesus, and when the Lord was about to be baptised the dove came down ; the Spirit came in the form of a dove and abode upon Him, as if He enjoyed the thought of being with the Lord Himself. And we surely ought to enjoy the thought. Brothers have written to me from several different parts of the world that they are getting great enjoyment out of the thought of the communion of the Holy Spirit ; that is one of the phrases that we get in the New Testament ; the love of God, and the fellowship or communion of the Holy Spirit. Then too we read of the love of the Spirit, and these are great things that in our secret histories it is our privilege to enjoy. We are to be happy instead of being downcast, or overcome by circumstances ; we are happy, for the Spirit is to shed abroad the love of God in our hearts, a very wide expression.

Ques. Would ministry like Ezekiel 47, have in view waters to swim in ?

J.T. Waters to swim in. There is no doubt that that might be a clue to what the Lord says in John 7 as to the Spirit, " as the scripture has said, out of his belly shall flow rivers." That probably alludes to Ezekiel 47. It is a wonderful chapter. We have not much more to say as to Revelation 3, it is a matter of what the Spirit says to the assemblies, and how much there is for us in what He is saying. It is the Spirit in ministry.

S.J.H. Could you give us some suggestion as to the titles we might use for the Holy Spirit in the morning meeting, whether we would start addressing Him as Lord and then if we were free use the different titles as we go on with the service ?

J.T. That would be a question of the intelligence you have, because the Scripture says, " the Lord is the Spirit " ; you can address the Spirit as Lord.

S.J.H. I thought that would be more for the early part, perhaps. Would it not be something different toward the end of the meeting ?

J.T. Perhaps so. The fact of the matter is that the subject is so large, the matter of the service of God is so large, that we might make mistakes if we spoke hurriedly, and our time is gone. We hardly know enough about the subject to apply it, and I am just a little afraid we might say something that would not be quite right. At the same time I do see that the term Lord is applicable to the Spirit of God, and it is applicable to the Lord Jesus Christ, and it is applicable to the Father ; He is sometimes called Lord, as in Matthew 11 : 25.

E.A.L. In regard to the repetition of the injunction to hear what the Spirit says to the assemblies, would it have a link with John 16 : 12 ; " I have yet many things to say to you, but ye cannot bear them now. But when he is come, the Spirit of truth, he shall guide you into all the truth." So that now it is not just a question of looking into the Scriptures and seeing a worded basis for what we should do, but rather as we are in the Spirit, He will show us what we should do and say ?

J.T. Just so, and I would add that the times we are living in now are greater than simply remnant times ; the Lord is bringing out fresh things for us from the Scriptures, or rather I should say the Spirit is doing it. The Lord said, " He shall show you things to come," and " He shall guide you into all the truth." We have not got all the truth, maybe we are getting some now.

Rem. Would the words of Haggai suggest that, his words that the latter glory of this house shall be greater than the former ?

J.T. That is a good confirmation, so that we might expect the latter glory to be greater than that at the beginning.

S.J.H. In the temple there were half-open flowers. Is there a suggestion that they are opening up now ?

J.T. That is right.

A.N.W. Does not John 7 show that there is more in the Scripture than we think there is ?

J.T. Well, it is wonderful, it is marvellous, the glories that are there ! " Hidden treasures " they are called, and we are to dig for those hidden treasures. We have not time, so we say. Maybe we say in the morning that we have to hurry away for a train ; but then these hidden treasures are more than a train, more than your business even ; we must attend to the Scriptures.

W.W. Do you not think one difficulty with us is that we want to stick to the letter of Scripture and not make way for the Spirit ?

J.T. Quite so, and yet we have the Spirit, who is ready to help us and to guide us ; it is a beautiful word, to *guide us into all the truth.*

W.W. So as we are amenable to the Spirit, He would open up these things to us.

J.T. He would indeed.

E.A.L. The Bereans searched the Scriptures to see if these things were so ; it does not say they searched them to see if they were not so. It is a positive approach.

J.T. It is the positive side, to see if these things were so. Why does it say that ? If the things available are so wonderful, why do we not just stop and think ? Maybe we shall get some wonders.

A.N.W. The Bereans received the things first, they did not refuse them, they received them.

J.T. They had a readiness of mind.

J.K.P. Is there not a beautiful suggestion of the present activities of the Holy Spirit as bringing out the full thoughts of God in 1 Corinthians 2 : 10, where it says that the Spirit searches all things, even the depths of God ? Do you not think we should cultivate more the desire for the company of the Holy Spirit in that way ?

J.T. I believe that God is honouring what the brethren have been doing. In Acts 20, seven brothers were concerned about things there. It was the first day of the week at Troas, and they had the Lord's supper, and Paul stood up to speak ; he discoursed as if there was a great deal to say, and I believe there is a great deal to say about this matter, and we had better be patient and hear it. They all listened to Paul till he finished, and then they went up and broke bread, and they went away comforted. That is the way things are ; that there is comfort.

S.McC. Do you think that verse 11 of chapter 3 is a good verse to go away with ? " I come quickly : hold fast what thou hast, that no one take thy crown." There is something distinctive about the Philadelphian phase.

J.T. Beautiful. And then the further great and glorious thought in the end of chapter 22, " And the Spirit and the bride say, Come." They say, *Come*, not, *Come quickly*, but *Come* ; as if the thing ought to be taken account of at once. The Lord is hearing that all the time, they are saying, *Come*. But over against that stands the patience of God.

THE WORSHIP OF GOD HIMSELF

ROMANS 11 : 33–36 ; 16 : 25–27 ; EPHESIANS 3 : 20–21

J.T. These scriptures record the deep feelings that moved the apostle in his writing, first in the epistle to the Romans and then in the epistle to the Ephesians. The consideration of them may serve under the Lord's hand to bring under review in a little way what immediately suggested the doxologies. We have first the ways of God on the earth as seen in Romans 10 and 11 ; then the Gospel itself as outlined in the epistle, leading to the closing verses where the mystery comes into evidence which is outside these ways. It comes into them but had been hid, and the subject of the epistle promotes such deep feelings as to call forth an ascription of praise to God in regard of the mystery. Then we have the unfolding of the mystery itself in Ephesians, leading to such feelings as are expressed in the few verses read, including the power that is available, the power in which God does " exceeding abundantly above all that we ask or think." This last passage is intended to fortify us in the maintenance of the exalted truths of the epistle.

C.A.C. Yes, indeed. Would you suggest that the spirit of these wonderful utterances is intended to pervade the service and worship of the assembly ?

J.T. I thought the consideration of them would lead us to the great end in view in all God's counsels and ways. In each case it is God, the ascription of praise is to God, God Himself being the great end ; God as such being the end in view. I believe that as we are drawing near to the end of this dispensation the Spirit would move in that way, that God should come before us feelingly ; for these ascriptions of praise are to Him because of what He is in Himself.

F.W.W. In what character do you view God in these doxologies ?

J.T. Well, briefly : the first scripture in Romans 11 alludes to His wisdom, knowledge and judgments as manifested in His ways, His sovereign ways, His sovereignty affecting not only His people but those who are not such ; then the second in chapter 16 is God in relation to the assembly, the establishing (verse 25) being needed by us, but the doxology going to God as such ; finally in Ephesians it is God as He is presented to us in John 1 : 18, for instance—" No one has seen God at any time ; the only-begotten Son, who is in the bosom of the Father, he hath declared him." So in Colossians, we have the Son spoken of as " image of the invisible God,"—Christ is that.

C.A.C. In what relation does that stand to the name of Father ?

J.T. Well, I have been thinking lately that these relations into which God has entered through the incarnation have in mind what we are ; it is God coming within the range of our intelligence and affections so as to secure us with a view to what He is in Himself. Having entered into the relation of Father with His Son, that relationship stands, but it is necessarily a narrower or more limited thought than the thought of Godhead, although the Father is God. The great thought is *God* ; that is the word the Spirit of God uses to convey the Deity. That is the great thought. The relation into which He has entered is not anything less blessed, for it involves our being brought near in relations suited to Him, not simply as creatures but as sons ; and all to the end that men might through redemption be brought near in freedom to worship God.

E.J.McB. You think of God as the supreme thought ?

J.T.   I think that is how Scripture presents the truth.

E.J.McB.   And as to these doxologies, would the first one be more a question of His judgments, and the second one more a question of His wisdom, and the final one what we might speak of as the greatness of God ? He is able to do all.

J.T.   Quite so, as regards what is available for our help ; and then, " To him be glory in the assembly in Christ Jesus unto all generations of the age of ages."   Ephesians gives us the full thought.

C.S.S.   Would that be suggested in Psalm 50 : " Out of Zion, the perfection of beauty, God hath shined " ?

J.T.   Quite so, the shining out of God. It is not now the shining out of His creation, but *He* shines out of Zion, the perfection of beauty. The first doxology here is, " Of him, and through him, and for him are all things " ; that is, the bearing of all this is Godward, as indeed we should expect in ascriptions of praise or worship. In unfolding these wonderful things by the Spirit, He knew the One who was capable of such emotions, reminding us that in ministry and service these emotions are in keeping. The ministry occasions them ; the servant is not only being used, but he is an intelligent person himself and capable of these emotions.

F.W.W.   These doxologies result from the spirit of worship in the speakers ?

J.T.   That is what I was thinking, that in unfolding these sovereign ways of God in relation to Israel the apostle is moved first as to the depths of wisdom ; the first doxology is occasioned by the thought of the depths of wisdom, that is the first thing mentioned : " O depth of riches both of the wisdom and knowledge of God ! "

Ques.   Would the title here be equivalent to the

title in the first chapter of Genesis, " In the beginning God " ?

J.T. I think so, I think that is what is in mind ; it is God. " In the beginning God . . ." The word is in the plural in Genesis 1, which would emphasise the thought of the Supreme, the One to be worshipped.

C.A.C. Are these ascriptions specially to be noted as being the only intimation of the character of worship on the part of the saints ? We have no account in the New Testament of expressions used in the assembly, have we ?

J.T. You mean that we have no Psalter in the New Testament, so we have to take these expressions as representative of what believers said in the early days. Yes, one can understand that if the apostle Paul were in a meeting on the first day of the week, as he would be as he had opportunity, he in worship to God would touch on these things. Of course, we rightly bring Christ and present Him to God in His infinite perfections as Son ; but then there is what God is, and that is touched on in these passages : " O depth of riches both of the wisdom and know-ledge of God ! How unsearchable his judgments, and untraceable his ways ! " You feel that the speaker is in the presence of God, the Source of all, for he proceeds to say, " Of him, and through him, and for him, are all things." He is in the presence of God ! He would be supported in this, of course, by the great Priest, for access to God is through the great Priest ; and he would be in the power of the Spirit ; but he is in the presence of God.

L.M. As to God and the Father, would you say why John in his gospel and epistles puts the two thoughts alongside so often ? For instance, in chapter 4, " The Father seeketh such to worship him " ; and then, " God is a Spirit ; and they that worship him must worship him in spirit and in truth."

J.T. While they run together, God is the great thought. " God is a Spirit." The Father is a relation entered into ; in John it usually denotes God in grace, that He has entered into that relation in grace, hence, " The Father judgeth no man," John 5 : 22. That shows in itself that it is a title or relation narrower, though not less blessed, than the primary or the final thought. God is the primary and the final thought. The relations taken are with a view to the great final thought being reached, that God might be known. See what a knowledge the worshipper has here ! What an apprehension of God he has ! How he is moved in thinking of Him, in the word, " O depth of riches both of the wisdom and knowledge of God ! " He is in the presence of God, he is in the presence of the great Being who has come out ; and he is moved in His presence and moved intelligently.

Ques. Is that the thought in 1 Corinthians 15 : 28 : " Then shall the Son also himself be subject unto him that put all things under him, that God may be all in all " ?

J.T. That is the end.

E.J.McB. Is this somewhat similar to Israel's blessing of Joseph's sons, where he refers to the God that had brought Abraham and Isaac through ? " The God before whom my fathers Abraham and Isaac walked, the God that shepherded me all my life long," Gen. 48 : 15. Is that the character of doxology, and should we not experience, as the result of God's ways with us, this holy sense of His own blessedness ?

J.T. That is what I think we might see, that the Spirit is aiming at that ; God is to be worshipped because of what He is Himself. Jacob alludes to the God of his fathers, and the God that shepherded him ; his view is very great for him. But when you come to Exodus 3 God not only says, " I am the

God of thy father," but when Moses makes the inquiry, Who shall I say sent me ? God says, " I AM." There you touch something that enters into this chapter ; " I AM hath sent me unto you," Ex. 6 : 14. That is the ever-existing One.

Ques. As to the word of the Lord, " I ascend unto my Father, and your Father ; and to my God, and your God," John 20 : 17, is God the higher thought there ?

J.T. God is necessarily the greatest thought. The Father comes first there, but it never comes first in the epistles. When you get the ascriptions, there it is to God and Father ; God is first, so that we have to take John 20 as progressive. That is, you come into the knowledge of the Father ; the Father is a term of the relationship into which He has brought us that we may know Him more intimately ; the very term implies that. There is more intimacy possible than with God as God, but that intimacy that we come into serves us in good stead in worshipping God. The relationship is to that end, it is progressive ; that in the knowledge of the Father I have power and more liberty to speak to God. I believe the Son in taking graciously a lower place on our account as Man, teaches us how to speak to God, gives us feelings, as in the case of the apostle here, suitable to God. The relation of Father and Son serves to that end.

Ques. Is God as thus presented the Source and Object of all in Romans ?

J.T. That is what is stated plainly here, and with a view to that we see how He acted sovereignly in chapter 9, not only in regard to Isaac, but also in regard to Jacob and Esau. He acted sovereignly as to Isaac and Jacob in regard of those born after the Spirit ; but He also acted sovereignly as to those who were not. He says, " Jacob have I loved, but Esau have I hated." We have to know God in that way. He did not say He hated Esau before he was born, but it is brought in in that connection. Before they were born He said, " The elder shall serve the younger." That is God's sovereign discrimination in favour of one person and against another. Then He raised up Pharaoh sovereignly to show His power in him.

T.C.F. Would you say that God has entered into a mediatorial position so that He might be known thus ?

J.T. The relationship and the system of affections are really to lead us into a state great enough to worship God ; not that the worship of God is any more blessed, but it is the end in view. Obviously the Creator is to be worshipped, the Supreme is to be worshipped.

Ques. Is that the idea of glory in each scripture ?

J.T. Exactly, the great end is God, and these relations set men free, set us free so that we might worship Him.

P.A.R. Would this doxology connect with Proverbs 8 in any way, the beginning of God's way there ?

J.T. I think so, wisdom is in mind in that chapter as marking His ways. That is the first thing mentioned in Romans, " O depth of riches both of the wisdom and knowledge of God ! "

G.C.S. In the song of Moses he says, " Ascribe ye greatness unto our God," Deut. 32 : 3.

J.T. Quite so, " greatness to our God."

C.S.S. Is your thought that these depths of God's riches are made known to the assembly, as we get, " The Spirit searches all things, even the depths of God " ; and He reveals them to us ?

J.T. He does, but this is really in a way greater, because it extends back to what was remarked as to Proverbs 8 ; it goes back to the beginning of God's way ; wisdom was there. Proverbs 8 takes us back to the beginning of everything, and wisdom was there ; that is, you are impressed with this, that God was operating, and He was operating in wisdom. So that all Scripture is intended to promote the knowledge of God in our hearts and minds, from Genesis 1 onwards. " In the beginning God " ; a great thought presented in a word that denotes supremacy and power, presented in the plural as if to remind us of God ; and that is never to be lost sight of. The whole tenor of Scripture is to keep that before us, to make us worshippers.

Ques. Is that what underlies the Lord's prayer in John 17 ?

J.T. The three chapters in Romans blend together in the apostle's mind by the Spirit. He begins with deep feeling as to Israel, as to those whom God took up sovereignly, showing that he is not a mere instrument but a feeling person, a man affected feelingly. He is a worshipper even in that matter. So deep are his feelings that he says, " I could wish that myself were accursed from Christ for my brethren, my kinsmen according to the flesh," Rom. 9 : 3. That is the feeling that the sovereign ways of God promote in us. He took up that people and the apostle gives us a list of things that attached to them : " Who are Israelites ; whose is the adoption, and the glory, and the covenants, and the law-giving, and the service, and the promises ; whose are the fathers ; and of whom, as according to flesh, is the Christ, who is over all, God blessed for ever. Amen," Rom. 9 : 4, 5. That is another doxology ; it is the outcome of his feelings, of what he is about to speak of as to Israel, a people that God took up sovereignly and in connection with whom is the Christ ; but who is He ? God, over all, blessed for ever. Now you may question why this as to God is brought in there. We come at the end of these three chapters, 9–11, to God, and praise ascribed to Him because of His wisdom, knowledge, judgments, and so on ; but this God is Christ too. Christ is God over all, blessed for ever. I mention that because of the importance of our being governed in our minds by Scripture's way of speaking ; lest there should be any shade cast on Christ. In making everything of God rightly there is not ; it is just that He has come in according to this wisdom, according to love of course, but according to such a scheme of wisdom ; that One who is spoken of as God over all should come in in connection with Israel and be known here as a Sufferer, a lowly Servant. But what for ? To the end that the great primary thought of God should be reached ; and it is reached in those verses read.

Ques. Does this first doxology suggest the entire solution of every moral question for God Himself, everything caused to work for His glory in that way ?

J.T. That is right ; all is for Him.

Rem. I thought this treatise on the Gospel comes in so that God gets His own pleasure out of man now, however viewed.

J.T. " Through him "—we have to understand how that works out ; I think the epistle has that in mind. At the beginning of these three chapters we see the wonderful scheme of wisdom, that Christ came in in relation to God's earthly people. Instead of bringing Him in immediately after Adam failed, wisdom required that centuries should pass by, and God should call out a people in connection with whom all these things should be, and then that Christ should be by them. Surely we have to consider wisdom in all that ! Wherein lies the wisdom of God postponing the incarnation ? He spoke of it in Genesis 3, and He postponed it for centuries ; and in the interim He calls out Abraham and Isaac and Jacob, and attaches to them the promises, the law and the adoption. He brings all these things in before the incarnation. What does all that mean? What have I gained by that? What is there in that lesson book for me? That is what enters into these chapters; and then finally the Christ, who is over all, God blessed for ever. There is the scheme of wisdom; the great lesson book for faith to understand and see how God reaches His thought in His ways on earth.

Ques. Is it not the sovereignty of mercy that the apostle is speaking of here? Having learned what mercy is, it fits us to think of God in this worshipping way.

J.T. That is right; that comes into it, the idea of wisdom is the first thing mentioned. He is rich in mercy to all that call upon Him; and Ephesians too, says He is rich in mercy; but then He is rich in wisdom. What does all this mean? Why did He defer the incarnation? What is He working out?

C.A.C. And it is all God; if it is through Him, it is through God, not exactly through the Mediator. Is that important?

J.T. "Through him"; that is the reason why it is well to call attention to what is said about Jesus at the beginning as, "over all, God blessed for ever." It is God's doing, and the One who carries it out in detail, the Man Christ Jesus, is no less than that; He is God.

T.C.F. Would you allow the suggestion that the thought of God in these doxologies is greater than that of God in Genesis 1?

J.T. It must be, for there we have the bare statement, "In the beginning God created the heavens and the earth"; but now we have the unfolding of wisdom in God's ways. Why did He defer the incarnation? He spoke of the seed of the woman coming in, but it was not immediate. All this is worked out in the meantime. What is it for? It is a question of wisdom, and as a lesson-book for us, so that we should be worshippers from this standpoint, so that we should know God from this standpoint ; so the three chapters go over the ground. The apostle in the first emotional statement tells us the depths of his feelings—what he thought of those whom God called out, Israel, as He called them. But what do I think about them ? It may be only a few years before God will begin to move in them ; what do I think about them ? The apostle says, What I think is this, that at one time I was ready to be accursed from Christ because of them ; and he tells us why. Then he proceeds to show how God in coming in in this way works sovereignly ; He took up Isaac instead of Ishmael ; He took up Jacob instead of Esau ; and so on. The principle of sovereignty comes home to me, Why did He take up me ? Any of us ought to be able to say that, Why did He take up me ? He passed by others. That is intended to make me a worshipper.

L.O.L. Is it significant that we do not read much of wisdom until we come to Solomon ? He asked for wisdom. Solomon wrote Proverbs 8.

J.T. You can see how great a thought wisdom is in Solomon, in God taking up a man and making him so wise. Wiser than all men ; wiser than Ethan, than Heman and Calcol ; he had no equal. Of course the thought is Christ : Christ now is the wisdom of God. But we can only touch on these things, they are really the greatest possible things ; the greatest range of things is what is presented in these doxologies. It may be the gain will be in the suggestion more than in what may be said.

When we come to the last chapter, the apostle has the mystery before him. Why did God keep it a mystery ? We are told in Proverbs 25 that it is the glory of God to conceal a matter, we have to understand wherein the glory lies ; the glory of concealment. So that what is in view is the establishment

of the brethren, of the saints, " according to my glad
tidings, and the preaching of Jesus Christ, according
to the revelation of the mystery, as to which silence
has been kept in the times of the ages, but which
has now been made manifest, and by prophetic
scriptures, according to commandment of the eternal
God, made known for obedience of faith to all the
nations—the only wise God, through Jesus Christ,
to whom be glory for ever. Amen." It is again a
question of wisdom. We have to see wherein lies
the glory of concealment, spoken of in the book of
wisdom, that is the book of Proverbs, and how there
was wisdom before the world, prepared for our
glory. See 1 Cor. 2 : 7.

H.P.W. It says here, " According to commandment of the eternal God." That links us with the
greatest thought of God.

J.T. Yes ; God, but now the eternal God.

C.A.C. Is that the thought of the mystery of God
in Colossians ? It is what pertains to the knowledge
of God Himself. " In which are hid all the treasures
of wisdom and of knowledge," Col. 2 : 3. It is a
greater and wider thought than the assembly, is it
not ?

J.T. That seems to be how it stands. The
mystery of God, I suppose, includes all that can be
called mystery. This thought of mystery is intended
to make us treasuries, hiding places, safe keeping
places or depositories for divine thoughts.

C.A.C. Then the apostle's agony of desire for
the saints in Colossians 2 stands in direct relation to
what you are bringing before us to-day.

J.T. He was combating. One feels how meagre
we are in dealing with these immense matters, but
yet they belong to us. One is made to feel one's
limitations and the limitations of the brethren ;
how little we can elucidate these thoughts, they are
so great and we are so limited ! The very suggestion

of these wonderful depths of God is so great, unveiling His mystery so that we may be rooted and grounded in love. It is the state of the saints that is in mind here. Even a Paul could not unfold the thing to certain ones because of their state. What God would remind us of is our state; whether there is the state of love and the unity of the Spirit, so that these things should be unfolded to us that we might know "the mystery of God; in which are hid all the treasures of wisdom and of knowledge."

E.J.McB. Would the thought be that if one accepts the sovereignty of God and the wisdom that has taken one up, one would want to be established in the present ministry and the place the assembly has in the mystery of God?

J.T. The epistle, I suppose, augments this; the apostle does not go forward to unfold it to the Romans, but it is the expected outcome that should be looked for by those who have received the gospel; "according to my gospel, and the preaching of Jesus Christ, according to the revelation of the mystery." It was already revealed; it does not speak of it as future, it was already there; but the Romans evidently were not ready for it. The establishment would be that we might be equal to the thing, to the mystery that he speaks of here, leading up to the great thought of God wherein are hidden all the treasures of wisdom and knowledge. They are hidden there; they are not spread abroad for the natural mind of man; they are hidden there.

C.A.C. Could we have a little on Ephesians 3.

J.T. Well, I thought it would be a good finish to our reading as leading up to the great end. The passage really begins immediately with the apostle's prayer to the Father that He would grant the saints to be strengthened by the Father's Spirit in the inner man. It is the Spirit of the Father, I apprehend, to the end that the Christ should dwell in our hearts by faith, that we being rooted and grounded in love, should be able to take in what is "the breadth and length and depth and height; and to know the love of the Christ." That is where we are led to, to this great thought, the strengthening by the Father's Spirit, that we might thus be fully able to know "what is the breadth and length and depth and height; and to know the love of the Christ which surpasses knowledge; that ye may be filled even to all the fulness of God"—not the Father here, but God. Then in verse 20 he says, "But to him that is able to do far exceedingly above all which we ask or think, according to the power which works in us, to him be glory in the assembly in Christ Jesus unto all generations of the age of ages." It seems as if we are led there to the final thought as to what God has in mind in the assembly.

Rem. The Father's Spirit would give us ability to apprehend Christ in His greatness: "Strengthened with power by his Spirit in the inner man; that Christ may dwell" in our hearts.

J.T. I think what you say suggests much. The relation entered into of Father and Son enables God to speak so as to be intelligible to us as to what He thinks of Christ, what His thoughts of Christ are. It is not simply God and man, it is Father and Son; and that is a relation that existed in humanity from the very beginning, and it is intelligible to us. "This is my beloved Son, in whom I am well pleased," Matt. 3 : 17, was the announcement from heaven; and that was said of a Man. Well, we are capable of understanding that. God works by way of environment with an end in view. He placed the relation of father and son in the human race; I do not think He placed it in the angelic order of being, although angels are called the sons of God. But I do not think Scripture warrants the thought that there is the relation of father and son amongst angels, that there is any suggestion of it. He is pleased to place that relation in the human race ; and all that God did had a purpose in it. He enters much more into detail than we are inclined to think, in view of taking us up according to His counsels. He operates externally : our antecedents, how we are brought up, our environment, all this is in God's mind. He works with wonderful forethought and detail in regard of each of us ; and if He had the idea of coming in in the relation of Father and Son, He places that relation amongst men. · It is well known. And so at the Jordan He announces from heaven, " This is my beloved Son, in whom I am well pleased." Anyone who heard that would be affected. There is the relation of Father and Son ; a Man being here on earth in that relation.

E.J.McB. And that is conducive to the knowledge of God in a worshipful way.

J.T. Conducive to the full thought that God had in mind.

C.A.C. So this scripture confirms the line of thought you have been suggesting ; the Spirit of the Father strengthening, and Christ dwelling in the heart through faith, leading up to the great thought of the fulness of God.

J.T. Yes ; that there may be glory to God in the assembly in Christ Jesus.

C.S.S. Do you think that the knowledge of the Son of God referred to in Ephesians 4 is preparatory to our being filled to all the fulness of God as in chapter 3 ?

J.T. I should think so, but of course in the epistle it comes afterwards in relation to ministry. All comes from the ascended Man, Christ in heaven, and the wisdom with which He has provided the ministers, as it is said, " for the work of the ministry, for the edifying of the body of Christ ;

till we all come in the unity of the faith, and of the knowledge of the Son of God, unto a perfect man, unto the measure of the stature of the fulness of Christ," Eph. 4 : 12, 13. You are alluding to that thought of the fulness of Christ. That fulness of Christ is one thing; what He is as Man in sonship, what comes out of that, as it were, that is what we are to come to. The fulness of God is obviously a greater thought although they run together. Being filled to all the fulness of God is, I apprehend, that the assembly is set up in the presence of God in the light of the full knowledge of God, not in the weakness of the creature; but in power filled unto all the fulness of God. I stand up there with all the saints as filled in the presence of God. Each of us would be there in that way.

A.J.G. Would that be the perfecting of the saints that you referred to at the beginning?

J.T. The perfecting of the saints comes in chapter 4, in the work of the ministry; the gifts are to that end, for the perfecting of the saints. That is to say, the saints are to be brought round to the full exercise of their senses; nothing missing, no malformation; so that there might be growth, growing up to Christ in all things. But then, "filled to all the fulness of God"; of course it is perfecting, but not the same thought, I think. The thought is, there is capacity formed; the saints are great persons. The Father's Spirit in the inner man implies capacity. I want to be able to take everything in that is there; and that is why we ought to be attentive now. The apostle says he bows his knees because of that; in Colossians he combats in view of the mystery of God, but here he bows his knees in view of capacity in the saints, that we may be fully able to take in the "breadth and length and depth and height; and to know the love of the Christ which surpasses knowledge." Think of the greatness of these things!

It is a question of capacity by the Father's Spirit in the inner man.

Ques. I was wondering whether the thought is seen in the sons of God in Job 38 : 7. The sons of God entered feelingly into what God was doing.

J.T. I think you can link that on with Paul here in Romans ; how they were moved when the foundations of the earth were laid ; the sons of God shouted for joy and the morning stars sang together. They entered sympathetically into what God was doing. With Paul, after the long history and manifestation of power on God's part, how beautiful it is to see him ascribe praise to God because of what He is ! Not only what Christ is—of course Christ is the manifestation of God—but then God is to be spoken to in relation to what He is Himself.

Ques. Have you the Holy Spirit in mind in relation to God ?

J.T. Certainly ; He is God Himself. God is here by the Spirit. That is why I was remarking that we should pay attention to the way Scripture speaks. We have in Genesis 1, " In the beginning God created the heavens and the earth " ; then, " And the earth was without form, and void ; and darkness was upon the face of the deep. And the Spirit of God moved upon the face of the waters." It is the same God but now He is moving in compassion, and that runs right through the history of the Spirit as we have it in the Scripture. It is what God is here compassionately and feelingly. God maintains His own majesty ; He is God, and yet He serves, and even makes coats for Adam. And right through it is God as feeling, even humbling Himself to behold the things in heaven and in the earth, Psa. 113 : 6. Yet He maintains His majesty in the Deity.

Rem. The heart of the apostle is bowed in the conscious sense of God's absolute supremacy.

J.T. That is what I was thinking. The apostle is

great enough to speak to God in this way ; and that is what one would like, to be great enough for such utterance. The passage is a matter of inward ability ; that we may be filled, able to take in these great things.

E.J.McB. We are to be competent to worship God intelligently.

J.T. And great enough in our feelings, not only to use the expressions, but great enough inwardly in ourselves in speaking to God. It is not only the question of intelligence, but of the spirit of wisdom and revelation in the knowledge of God ; that is Ephesians 1. Then the Father's Spirit in the inner man giving me ability to stand up in the presence of all this, and to enjoy it ; and to speak of it feelingly as Paul does here. You can see what a man Paul was by the Spirit, as able to speak in this way, and with such fulness.